"Q: "Who shall find a valiant woman?" (Proverbs 31:10)
A: The reader of this book.
The gripping story of Jan Haas' struggle to live reminds us that miracles weren't simply quaint medieval happenings. They still occur today."

Kathy Coffey, author of *Hidden Women of the Gospels, The Art of Faith* and *God in the Moment: Making Everyday a Prayer*

"This soulful experience of Jan's year-long journey with illness will touch others as they live and discover meaning in their own life stories. This is a book about healing and walking through life with deep breaths."

J.A. Heinlein,
Publishing/Media Marketing Professional

Jan's journey reminds us that the human body is capable of anything if we are patient and focused on the task at hand. She takes us up her mountain one step at a time. When you finish the book you will feel as though you have reached the top of the world right beside Jan."

Tonya Clement, Founder, Beyond Everest
20th U.S. woman to climb Mt. Everest and the fifth of just nine American women to reach the top of via the treacherous North Ridge.

"This riveting story of a mother fighting to live for her young family will inspire you to move through your life struggles. Her journey will have you crying, laughing, and wondering in awe about the power of community and prayer. Reading this book will leave you feeling hopeful and grateful. You'll want to pass it on."

Shelly Moorman, Parent Coach and Speaker,
Head and Heart Parent

"If you have the strength, follow this story from beginning to end. Embrace the agonies of the patient. Follow her family members as they prepare to lose her, and then face the exhausting challenge of keeping her alive. There is resurrection here. Let the stone roll away from your own horrors of hospitals and those who struggle there. Mountains are being moved even now, by the love stronger than death of all who companion their beloveds through the tunnel and back."

Kathy McGovern,
www.thestoryandyou.com

"This book portrays the shock, pain, and profound suffering of a woman and her family when an unexpected illness crashes into their lives. While Jan struggles to survive a rare infection that is often deadly, a network of medical staff and a community of love work to sustain this young family. Jan's illness transforms and brings meaning to her life today. Medical professionals can learn valuable lessons in the pages of her reflections."

Matt McCoy, MD

Moving Mountains

One Woman's Fight to Live Again

Jan Haas

www.movingmountainsbook.co

Cover Design: Melissa Levad
Cover Photograph: Teri Virbickis
www.adventuresbehindthecamera.com
Author Photograph: Tricia Turpenoff
www.turpenoff.com
Editing: Donna Mazzitelli
Layout Design: Andrea Costantine

Printed in the United States of America

First Edition
ISBN 978-0-9846933-0-6

Contents

Based on the journals
and writings of
Jan Haas

Journal entries by Tony Haas and Dorothy Wilson
Additional writings by community members

Dedicated...

To the committed medical professionals—doctors, nurses, lab technicians and therapists who rallied around me and helped me survive.

To the community of friends and family who did the work of providing prayer, food, friendship and sustenance for the long journey.

To my mom and dad, whose deep love I only understood after becoming a parent to my own three daughters.

To Becca, Hannah and Sarah whose passion for life and desire to make the world a better place are such joys in my life. You are the reason I fought to be alive today. It is through your love and wisdom that I continue the journey toward loving myself.

And, not least, to my best friend Tony, the man I married 25 years ago and the man with whom I find myself falling more deeply in love with each day. While his voice may not be loud in this book, his presence was and is felt daily by my side as we walk this journey, providing for me, raising our daughters, and shining like a beacon of hope for all to see.

The girls and I are Tony's living, breathing book. We are the masterpiece he is so proudly applauding from the back of the room.

And I am forever grateful.

Bloom

My words, like seeds,
lie dormant in the dark.
Each day I observe,
and any movement
is invisible to
the naked eye.

I can't force my words—
bring them inside to warm
and pretend it is spring.

Writing—
like life—
is an organic, earthy
process:
I must trust
the chaos of
darkness where
words root
and gradually sprout.
I dig in the dirt,
weed out,
nurture tender shoots.

And in the moment
I least suspect,
words bloom into form
and beauty.

Jan Haas

Foreword
By Kelly Gaul APRN-BC

I met Jan Haas approximately 16 years ago after she was admitted to the hospital where I worked as a Psychiatric Consultation Liaison Nurse. Jan developed an invasive strep A infection and toxic shock following the uneventful birth of her third child. Bad things do indeed happen to good people. She had five surgeries within the first 30 days and spent months in the hospital—much of that time in the Surgical Intensive Care Unit on a ventilator—only to return at a later date for more surgery. Through this, Jan touched many lives, including my own.

During the course of her prolonged illness and ultimate recovery, Jan endured anything and everything these kinds of critical illnesses confront us with, and she did so with courage and faith that inspired many people—her family, community, and those of us who had the great good fortune to care for her. I do believe meaning is found in reflection, and that is true for all of us as much as it is for Jan. It is also what makes this story all the more poignant and important for others who suffer similar challenges in life. Jan's account of the slog of her everyday experience—the inches, not the miles, the disappointments and the hope—is powerful, as are the descriptions of the relationships that made her recovery possible.

Jan has much to offer, and much has already been given. Those of us who have dedicated our lives to helping others, who walked the steps with Jan, if only for a little while, carry the image of a valiant young woman who reminded us and reminds us still of why we do what we do and how much it matters.

Melody Chenevert wrote, "In the end, we will not remember the years we spent in nursing. We will only remember the moments."

Jan Haas is the moment we will remember.

Introduction

I don't know why you picked up this book. Chances are you don't know me, but maybe the title grabbed your attention. Maybe you were part of the prayer circle that sustained me during my long illness. Maybe you brought meals or offered your friendship. Whoever you are, wherever you come from, my guess is there have been mountains in your own life, obstacles you have overcome to be the person you are.

This book is about a huge mountain—an illness that nearly took my life, but in return, gave me a new perspective on what it means to truly live. Through journals and reflection, I tell the story of how this illness became a blessing in my life.

The well of my faith has deepened over the years, nurtured by the love and care of many people and a belief that I am a part of Divine Wisdom, never separate from the One Great Love that sustains us all. Although God has always been a part of my life, finding peace in the arms of Mother God gave me the strength to continue the healing journey. My faith may have been of mustard seed size, but I don't believe faith moved the mountain of illness. Rather, like our friend Fr. Patrick Dolan says, faith gives us the courage to pick up the shovel and move the mountain ourselves. Many people picked up their shovels on behalf of our family and held us in prayer, cooked meals, washed laundry, and did whatever needed to be done. Moving mountains became a community-wide event. Faith in action was proof that God's love went far beyond my own understanding.

The journey through my year of illness is raw and difficult. I have kept my journals true to my voice during that time when depression had set in and God seemed far away. You will hear my voice wishing for "all this to end." Yet people and events kept appearing at the right time to remind me of a Divine Presence that wrapped around me and never left.

My mother's voice, from her own journal, carries us through the first part of the story. **You will see a few entries from my husband, Tony. They are distinguished with a slightly bolder font than my mother's, used above and shown here.**

There is a long list of characters in the book, and I have tried to describe them so that you can place how they came into my life, but here is the short list for your reference.

Tony - my husband and best friend

Becca, Hannah and Sarah - our daughters who at the time were five years old, two and a half, and a newborn.

Dorothy and Keith - my mom and dad

Fran - Tony's mom

Fran and Carol - Tony's dad and his wife

Mary Beth and Jeff - Tony's sister and her husband

Father Ken Koehler - Pastor of Most Precious Blood Church and Tony's boss

Rita Mailander - Becca's preschool teacher and later Religious Education Director at Most Precious Blood Church.

Kelly Gaul - Psychiatric nurse who followed my case

Brenda Foster - ICU nurse who became a friend

Dr. M - primary care doctor

Dr. P - primary surgeon

Sherlock - gastroenterologist

My story is woven together with dated journal entries and reflections. Reflective pieces are noted with indention and start with CAPITAL LETTERS. I have heard it said that our lives are lived forward and understood backwards. These reflections on the past help me understand myself more fully in the present, bringing healing across the years.

As a young girl, writing poetry was my way of dealing with typical teenage drama. I could get lost for hours in my room, writing in my journal and creating poetry that now only I can appreciate. The more I wrote, the more I dreamed of writing a book by the age of 30. While I didn't accomplish that goal, I am now completing a book about the story that took place when I was 30 years old. I am seeing my dream come to fruition. I began writing this book for my own healing, discovering the lessons of the past and their impact on the present. But the more I share my experience with others, the more I understand how my story is a metaphor for the challenges many people face.

Wherever you are on your journey, whatever kind of mountain you are moving, may this book be a source of strength and encouragement for you. Take time to breathe into the moment, and as you walk this journey with me, know that you too can take baby steps and arrive at a new place, even if it is only a new state of mind. With determination, connection to Divine Wisdom, and friends along the way, you are sure to reach your goal. You too can move mountains.

It's like the great stories Mr. Frodo. The ones that really mattered. Full of darkness and danger they were. And sometimes you didn't want to know the end because how could the end be happy? How could the world go back to the way it was when so much bad had happened? But in the end, it's only a passing thing, this shadow. Even darkness must pass. A new day will come. And when the sun shines, it will shine out the clearer. Those were the stories that stayed with you and meant something, even if you were too small to understand why. But I think, Mr. Frodo, I do understand. I know now. Folk in those stories had lots of chances of turning back only they didn't. They kept going because they were holding on to something.

What are we holding onto Sam?

That there is some good in this world, Mr. Frodo, and it's worth fighting for.

Samwise Gamgee
The Lord of the Rings, Two Towers

Saving a Life

I had just settled into my bed of pillows for the night when there was a knock at the open door. It was strange, because in the hospital I was used to people looking in on me at all hours of the day and night. Knocking before entering was not a normal approach.

I wasn't frightened as the stranger approached my bed. His scrubs and familiarity of procedures gave me an indication he was supposed to be there. When I looked up, I could see the tears rolling down his face. "Do you know who I am?" he asked.

"No," I responded, growing more curious by the moment.

"You died on the table during surgery. I am the one who got up on your chest and pounded on your heart to make it start beating again. I just can't believe you are here."

And sometimes, when I look back at what I survived, neither can I.

Birth

No one who has ever brought up a child
can doubt for a moment that love
is literally the life-giving fluid of human existence.

Smiley Blanton

The Birth of Sarah

Never underestimate the power of a mother's love that can carry her considerable distances when the need is great.
Jan Haas

January 21, 1995
Journal (five days before Sarah's birth)

So, little one, what do you look like? Will you be fair like Hannah or have a dark complexion like your sister Becca? Will you have brown eyes like me or green eyes to match your dad? And what joys and sorrows lie ahead of us? You bring us now the gift of wonder and the magical miracle of new life. I sit and wait, knowing that a miracle begun nine months ago in my womb will take full life in a few days.

What a gift you already are to me, little one, making me slow down. Thank you for giving me a moment to cherish the life within me before becoming a beautiful new bundle of baby joy in my arms. God has truly blessed me.

A belly full of life,
moving, bulging in strange places.

I try to grab a foot
or a hand
and make contact with you.

You tease me, you know,
playing this waiting game,
knowing full well when you intend
to make your earthly appearance.
But you keep me in the dark,
guessing.

I feel my uterus contract, and you squirm.
Is this the One? No
Is now the time? No

In your other worldly wisdom you say,
"Have a glass of wine Mom, relax!
My time will come soon enough."

You laugh at me and cause my belly to wiggle.
I poke and prod at you to pay you back.
See, our relationship has already begun!

OUR FIRST TWO dAUGHTERS, BECCA AND HANNAH, were born into our little church community in Cedar Rapids, Iowa. Tony's first job as a liturgist took us there, where I found a job teaching fifth grade at a Catholic school.

We always said that Cedar Rapids was a great place to live, but you wouldn't want to visit. I mean, who can be excited about a bunch of corn fields? But the Cedar River in autumn was a beautiful sight. Its oak and maple-lined banks, ablaze with red and gold, held a magic all its own. Our lives were exciting as we met new people and learned the skills necessary for our new jobs. I shared stories of kids and the crazy things they say and do, and Tony learned how to deal with many personalities in his first church job. I sang in the adult choir, and most of our friends were rooted in our church community.

We settled into our first little two-bedroom bungalow and started our family. At a church gathering, when I was pregnant with Becca, we met a wonderful couple, Mary and Kevin Gesing. They had two daughters at the time, Emily and Abbey. Abbey was only six months old when Becca was born, so they became playmates and Mary and I became close friends.

Sharing meals at least once a week, we often relied on Mary and Kevin's experience to get us through the challenges of new parenthood. Experiencing life through the big brown eyes of a small child was a delight, and I found God in the midst of peanut butter sandwiches, hot cups of tea, lazy afternoons, and the laughter of little girls playing house.

Along with other choir and church members, we made a little church, a nurturing community inside the larger church in which all of us experienced the love and power of belonging. It was enriching for our marriage and for our family life. Hannah was also brought into this same community, although we moved when she was eight months old, as a yearning to be closer to grandparents and the Colorado mountains called us home. The bonds of friendship that were forged during those five years in Iowa remained a source of strength for me.

Tony's job as Liturgist and Music Director at Most Precious Blood Church created a new community for us. I trained as a member of the grief ministry team, and we joined a small Christian community consisting of mostly young married couples. It was into this small and large church that Sarah would be born and welcomed. I didn't know what powerful prayer warriors our small group and larger community could be. I would soon be held up in more prayer than I knew was possible.

❧

Sarah's birth was short and sweet. I wasn't expecting a long labor, since Becca came into the world after a four-hour labor, and Hannah graced us with her presence in less than three. Besides, I was already five centimeters dilated and one hundred percent effaced when I went to the doctor's office on a Thursday afternoon in January. I was feeling intense pressure because, as the midwife explained, the baby was acting like a cork, sitting low in my pelvis. The midwife didn't want to scratch Sarah's head!

My mom Dorothy was excited about being present at a grandchild's birth. Mary Beth, Tony's sister, coached our four-and-a-half-year-old daughter Becca through the birth. Packages of saltines kept her interest in the first few minutes. I can still see her in a jean jumper and pigtails, eyes wide open and licking an orange Popsicle, waiting for a little sister or brother to arrive.

Shortly after Seinfeld, the midwife arrived and carefully broke the bag of water that cushioned Sarah's head. Labor had officially begun. Tony and I walked the halls, peered at babies in the nursery, and felt very relaxed. My first contraction came at 9:15 p.m., and I sat in a hot shower, water releasing tension from my body. At 9:30 p.m., I climbed back into bed, and shortly before the ten o'clock news, Tony caught Sarah Elizabeth in his arms. He said she felt like velvet. He laid Sarah on my chest, and I got to enjoy the miracle of new life for 30 minutes before they whisked Sarah away to weigh her. Little did I know that over the next days, my time to hold, cuddle, and feed her would be cut short.

Insurance companies routinely sent new moms and babies home in less than 24 hours, so I was already home by three o'clock Friday afternoon. Post-partum days had been the hardest part of my previous two pregnancies, so when I didn't feel well on Friday night it seemed normal for me. I was happy to be home surrounded by family.

On Saturday, I felt weak. I conversed with the midwife about how I might regain my strength. Our focus was to relieve the pain in my back which prevented me from sleeping. Each movement I made felt as if I was rolling on a bed of rocks. I slept on the couch, not wanting to wake Tony. On Sunday, I remember my brother installing a new oven in our kitchen. Yet, I don't remember any time spent nursing or holding Sarah. I don't remember seeing Becca or Hannah, excited about their new little sister. I was so wrapped up in not being myself that I have no memory of bonding with Sarah those first days after her birth.

By the following Monday morning, I was no better, so I went to see the midwife. She checked my uterus and noted that it was tender, as it should be after delivery, but she gave me a round of antibiotics to start immediately, just in case there was an infection. I was to let her know the next morning if I noticed any change.

When I got up Tuesday, I was feeling extremely lightheaded and dehydrated. Before I could call the midwife, she called me. Hearing that my condition had not improved, she immediately sent me to her cooperating OB-GYN, who asked me to go the hospital for blood and urine tests and then come in for an office visit.

There was Tony, a baby in one hand and a wife unsteady on her feet, clinging to his other arm as he guided me to the hospital lab. I was so weak I had to lie down while the lab assistant drew my blood. After a 30-minute rest and a ride in a wheelchair to the car, we traveled three miles to the doctor's office, just in time for me to faint on the way into an examination room. It was a quick ride back to the hospital, where I remember with great amazement meeting my mother in the emergency room.

The phone calls over the weekend left my mother concerned. She had a sinking feeling that something was wrong with me, and it was her encouragement that pushed me to follow up with the doctor. When she didn't reach me by phone Tuesday morning, she immediately left work and drove to our house in Denver.

Her intuition told her she needed to find me. She called the doctor's office number on the new prescription bottle she'd found on our kitchen table, only to discover I was already on my way to the hospital. Seeing my mother and the look of concern on her face was the last thing I remember until almost five weeks later.

The Telling Signs
Dr. Matt McCoy

I was called out of an office exam room early one morning in January of 1995. On the phone was an obstetrician, unknown to me, who described the unconscious woman on the floor of his waiting room. He had called 911, was awaiting their arrival and wanted to consult. When the obstetrician reported that her pulse was so fast he couldn't count it, I knew our patient was either bleeding internally or septic with infection. Either diagnosis was life threatening and required immediate attention. I left my scheduled office patients to find her in the ER awake but weak, pale and short of breath, but somehow polite and remarkably calm. If one didn't already know, the results of the blood gas told just how sick she was—her body was already full of the acid of septic shock and overwhelming infection.

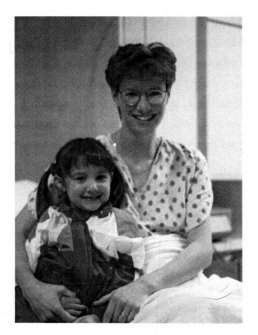

Awaiting Sarah's Birth with Five Year Old Becca

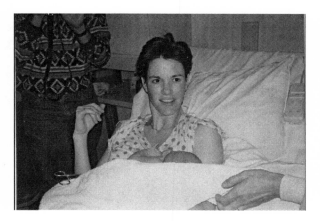

A New Baby in My Arms

Darkness

Catastrophe is the essence of the spiritual path;
it is a series of breakdowns allowing us to discover the
threads that weave all of life into a whole cloth.

Joan Halifax

A Mother's Despair

Dorothy (Mom's Journal)
Tuesday, January 31st, 1995, Day 1

When I got to the hospital, the nurse was frantically trying to get Jan's blood pressure. She called for an ER doctor who came in and found a femoral pulse. Jan felt cold and was "white as a sheet" and wondered why I was there. The doctors thought Jan had a massive infection, so they put her in Medical ICU.

Things are such a blur. So many specialists—so many ideas. A lactation nurse to pump Jan's breasts, but they couldn't keep the milk because of the antibiotics. An infectious disease specialist. A pulmonologist. They wanted to get Jan into a program for an experimental medication that would help clear the blood of toxins. The doctors decided to intubate her during the night because she was having more and more difficulty breathing. I remember saying, "She could die!"

Father Ken came in to anoint Jan at Tony's request. Tony's mother Fran came in at the time Jan's blood pressure had gone down to 40 and they were fighting to restore it. When Tony got back upstairs, the curtain was drawn and he could not get back into the room.

Mom's Journal,
Wednesday, February 1, Day 2

Dr. W found me in the hall and said things didn't look good. Things had not gone well during the night, and perhaps it was time to gather the family together and start praying (as if we hadn't been). Tony and I talked for a while about the seriousness of the situation. I think it was very difficult for us to face the fact that we might have to let Jan go!

Dr. G, a GYN infection specialist, was called in. He advised an immediate hysterectomy. At 2:30 p.m., Jan went into surgery. I remember crying and thinking that I might never see Jan again. But as I was praying, I had a vision of Jan and she said, "I will be back, Mom. I'm OK." It made me feel much better then, but as time went on that vision faded.

After a couple of hours, Dr. W came in and told us that they had taken the uterus and ovaries—they were very infected—and then general surgeons looked over the rest of the abdomen to see if anything else was going on. Although Jan made it through, they had to take most of her colon and her gallbladder. The colon was "dead" and the gallbladder looked bad, so they took it out.

The doctors told us that Jan has a massive infection caused by an invasive strep A bacteria that is releasing its poisons into her bloodstream and organs. The statistics aren't good for Jan to survive this.

One of the drugs Jan is taking is called Levophed, and I heard the nurses using the tagline, "Levophed or dead." It works to increase the blood flow to the heart and other vital organs while constricting blood flow to less important peripheral parts of the body. It is only used in the most extreme cases when there are few options.

The general surgeons also said the small bowel looked

questionable—there were lots of places in it that looked suspicious, but they were planning to take Jan back to surgery the next day for another look. They do that to give the bowel a chance to get better. Jan has a temporary iliostomy. The end of her small intestine (ileum) was brought through the abdominal wall to form a stoma, or a temporary anus, where bodily wastes will be excreted. An external pouch will be stuck to her skin to collect waste. When her body heals, they can reconnect the ends of the intestines. We were very thankful that she had made it through this long day of surgery.

Father Ken came up that night and spent some time with Tony and me in the consultation room. Jan always said her biggest fear was for something to happen to Tony and for her to be left alone. Now Tony faced being a single parent, a widower at the age of 31 with three children. Ken told us about an experience he has never forgotten from his early years in which his mother "died" and came back. She was told she had children to raise and she couldn't get into heaven yet. We were certainly hoping Jan would be there to raise her children. Ken prayed with us before he left, and we slept in that room for the night.

Mom's Journal,
Thursday, February 2nd, Day 3

The resident surgeon said the head of every department in the hospital was in Jan's room. One of the doctors said he was amazed that so many egos were in check and they were actually agreeing on a plan for Jan's best chance at survival. I again watched as they wheeled Jan away, dreading all the possibilities. Would she make it through the second surgery? Would they have to remove the small bowel? We all have about thirty feet of small bowel, and they said we have to have at least two feet to be able to digest food. If she didn't keep that much, she would have to be fed intravenously the rest of her life.

We were scared! And as we had so often before, we prayed. After a couple of hours, Dr. B came back and said they only had to take six inches of small bowel. The rest didn't look real good. But they flushed it out and used some kind of fluorescence to see through it all and it looked OK. We were so relieved and felt that we had hit a high point. Our relief was so great that we allowed ourselves to get too optimistic. Tony and his sister, Mary Beth, were the only ones who stayed on a more level ground, being very cautious and not getting their hopes up. We found out they were right.

Before everyone left that day, we prayed together. I think our prayers were beginning to lean more toward praying for God's will— not ours—that God loves Jan more than we do and that we were so grateful for His blessings and help and miracles so far, but we wanted what was best for Jan, whatever that might be.

Tony's Journal,
February 2nd

This week has been one of the best and one of the worst for me. The support of community and family has been great. But at times I feel like I am at a wedding reception that I cannot leave, having to spend time with each person. This, more than anything, will wear me out. Since Tuesday, each day has been a blur. I want to write down what I remember before my days become more of a blur...

> Call it a clan, call it a network, call it a tribe, call it a family. Whatever you call it, whoever you are, you need one.
> - Jane Howard

When we got to Dr. W's office, I filled out the paperwork. We went to a room and Jan fainted. Dr. W could not get a blood pressure and had the nurse call 911. I felt so helpless at that moment. Jan was lying on the floor, and Sarah was in my arms. I didn't know what to do, so I cried.

The intern, Dr. W, is caring, has a great bedside manner, and is informative. He stayed with us for the first 36 hours and visited on a regular basis, even when he was not on duty.

Prayer Circles
Judy Burton, retired Most Precious Blood Church parish secretary

I was working at the parish office and we heard that Jan's condition was worsening rapidly. I went over to the church to pray. I cried and asked God, "Please don't let this happen to this family." More tears. When I sat down in the pew to compose myself to return to work, I had the most comforting and peaceful feeling come over me. I knew to trust that Jan would be with her family again. Someone who worked with my husband said prayers were being said for Jan at his parish too. I think every parish in the city was praying for her.

Mom's Journal,
Friday, February 3rd, Day 4

At midnight, Tony came into the waiting area and woke me up. They were taking Jan back to surgery—her abdomen was filling up again. Her blood was producing acid and they couldn't get a normal blood pressure. I was scared to death! Three surgeries! They had given her zero chance to live without surgery and only a 20% chance to make it through the first surgery. I didn't know what her chances had been for the second surgery but I surely didn't believe they were very confident going in the third time!

About fifteen minutes after they went into the operating room with Jan, I heard someone in the hall say there was a cardiac arrest in surgery and I just knew it was Jan. I was so frightened—I just sat and prayed. Jan had arrested—they had to shock her heart but got a heartbeat again. The surgeons opened her abdomen and as soon as they did, her blood pressure stabilized. The toxins were still causing swelling, so they cut open an IV bag and sewed the plastic over the abdominal opening so there would be room for swelling. They would leave it that way for a while.

Jan's body is so swollen with the infection that her hands look like blown-up surgical gloves, and I can only see the ends of her eyelashes poking out from her puffy face. It doesn't look like Jan at all and it is hard to watch.

Choosing Life

Floating in white space,
deaf to any sound around me.

There is no pain, no struggle.
I feel nothing
except a warm peace flooding through me
and an overwhelming curiosity.

Where am I?
How did I get here?

I have no sense of body,
no place where I end and
everything else begins.
I am limitless space.

My human mind

rearranges molecules
until I am seated in a chair
high above an operating room,
the sole observer
to the trauma below.

My body shell is draped in cloth,
exposed belly splayed open.
I watch in muted slow motion
the flurry of activity
as a surgeon
climbs onto the table
and with all his strength
pounds the beat back into my heart.

A thin veil
separates the place between
the stillness of death
and the uncertainty of life.

Is the doctor hammering my physical heart
or awakening my will to live?
Is it one in the same?

Tony's Journal
Saturday, February 4th

As I am sitting here writing, one of Jan's nurses asked me if I was writing my memories. I told her I was trying to remember the events of the past few days, but they were getting fuzzy. She asked if I really wanted to remember all that has happened. I told her that I didn't have a choice. I have to remember: for my sake as I try to understand how and why this is happening; for Jan's sake so she may know what has happened, and for the girl's sake, so they know what took place. Life is difficult and running from the pain of all of this will not help anyone.

How Do I Pray?
Lori Johnston, Jan's cousin

I don't remember when my Mom called. I just remember hearing her voice shake. "Jan's in the Intensive Care Unit. They are not sure she's going to make it." It was very surreal. Mom, my sister Sheri and I went to the hospital right after Jan's third surgery. We could go into Jan's room one at a time. My mom was very calm. She held Jan's hand and talked to her. Jan was so bloated with fluids; it really didn't look like her. Aunt Dorothy was there, of course. I don't think she ever left Jan's side. Then we went to the hospital chapel to pray. I sat there thinking, "What do I ask God for? Strength for Tony? Wisdom for the doctors? What do I ask for?" I remembered of all the happy memories—time we spent with Jan and Tony, times we watched Becca and Hannah, playing games, and sharing a meal. I thought that if Jan could feel the love surrounding her, surely she would be healed. From that moment on, every time I thought about Jan, I sent love her way. I wanted her to feel a wave of love flowing over her at all times.

Tony's Journal,
Saturday, February 4th, Day 5

Since the surgeries, Jan's condition has remained mostly unchanged. The doctors try to wean her off the blood pressure medications but her body is not cooperating. Every time the medication is lowered, her blood pressure drops.

We had one crisis yesterday. The doctors were watching two red spots on her hip and knee. The one on the hip grew quite a bit in two hours' time. It was also hot and sensitive to the touch. The doctors were concerned because the invasive strep A bacteria is known to move out of the blood stream and hide in muscles where it waits to rear its ugly head again. They were worried this might be the case and that the infection had re-emerged and was now in the body tissue. If this was the case, they would have to remove all the infected tissue and cut off a limb. Luckily, it was not the case. They made an incision into Jan's hip and the tissue bled and looked healthy.

Right now, I am trying to live from one crisis to the next. One doctor told me to divide my days into six- to eight-hour increments, and if we made it through one increment without incident, we were OK. I have done this. Jan is a long way from being well. It will be a real test of my endurance. Another doctor told me she is by far the sickest person in this hospital. My first thought was, "This must not be a very big hospital." I was shocked to hear such news.

My prayer for the last few days has been to ask for strength and the wisdom to deal with whatever the future brings. I hope I am able to rise to the occasion.

Mom's Journal,

Saturday, February 4th, Day 5

Down to the depths again! How much can she take? How many assaults can her body take? We pray again—that we can accept what is best for Jan. We want her with us, of course, but we also want a quality life for her. We put her in God's hands.

We will probably never know how many people have been affected by Jan's illness. Everyone we talk with thinks about her almost constantly. Everyone looks at this family and sees themselves. They wonder how in God's name they could cope with such a catastrophe. Even the doctors and nurses have become emotionally involved. They look at Jan and see a member of their family. They constantly comment on the strength shown by our family and about how strong a person Jan must be to have survived this and to keep fighting.

The Beginning of Love

COLORADO SNOW-CAPPED PEAKS AND LAYERS OF MOUNTAINS are a part of my everyday life in Denver. Lucky for me, my main travel route to most anywhere I drive frequently heads west, and as I reach the highway, the mountains stand up from the ground in full splendor, pulling me into a space of gratitude for their beauty and strength. As long as I can remember, mountains have always made their presence known in my life.

I grew up in Fort Collins, Colorado against the backdrop of Horsetooth Mountain. The bold A for Colorado A&M, or Colorado State University which it later became, was made of white rocks laid out in a pattern on the side of the hill. Every day I looked to those mountains, and spotting the A, felt grounded in a sense of place. Fort Collins was home.

I was the youngest of three children, the only girl with two older brothers. My mother worked full time as an x-ray technician and was a full-time mom too. My father worked in the car business, learning the trade at his own father's gas station. Whether it was auto parts sales or car sales, he worked hard to bring home a living for his family.

For my elementary years, I attended St. Joseph's Catholic School. It was a time when nuns in black habits and white coifs still ruled the school, yet most of my teachers were not part of the religious order. My first grade teacher was Sister Ann Dominic, and I loved the big round curves of her body hidden under yards of draped material. She seemed to float through the halls with grace. I was in favor with her, earning the right to have free afternoons because of good behavior. Who wanted to read about Dick and Jane when, with enough stamped stars on my work chart, I could spend time in the creative corner of the large coat closet that ran the length of the classroom? My art paper attached easily to a magic easel splashed with a multitude of hues, and I dipped my brush into tubs of primary colors, painting pictures that stretched my imagination and kindled my creativity.

For religion class, we recited our answers to the Baltimore Catechism. 1. Who made us? God made us. 2. Who is God? God is the Supreme Being, infinitely perfect, who made all things and keeps them in existence. 3. Why did God make us? God made us to show forth His goodness and to share with us His everlasting happiness in heaven. 4. What must we do to gain the happiness of heaven? To gain the happiness of heaven we must know, love, and serve God in this world. (Lesson One)

Once a year in February, on the Feast of Saint Blase, the priest of the parish would come into the school and bless all of the children by touching two candles on either side of the throat. "Through the intercession of Saint Blase, bishop and martyr, may God deliver you from every disease of the throat and from every other illness." What was it that passed through those candles and warmed the back of my throat? Did the priest have some special powers because of his relationship to God? From my six-year-old eyes, the rituals and formalities of the Catholic Church were filled with a magic I couldn't explain. I didn't understand the significance of the Eucharist, the power of the Holy Spirit to move through our world. I don't understand them fully today. But what I did know was the feeling of belonging in community, and the sense of peace that would come over me when I said my prayers. Those were the intangible things, the mysteries I could hold on to.

I was in Catholic school shortly after the time of the Second Vatican Council, when, among many other changes, the words of the mass were changed from Latin to English. My fourth grade teacher played her guitar for the school masses, a nice change from the organ music I was used to. When I showed her a poem I wrote about God, she put it to music. With her guitar strumming in the background, I sang my song in front of the school. I remember the trepidation in my voice when the first line came out of my mouth, but with an encouraging nod and a smile, my voice became stronger, singing out with a power I didn't know existed within me.

About this time, we moved to a new house farther away from downtown, next door to my best friend Dian, whom I had met in third grade. Every morning, we took the city bus to school. As we waited for the afternoon bus to ride home, we befriended the principal, Sister Ann Mueller. We helped her with errands, feeling important in the carrying out of small tasks. Sometimes she would share cookies with us. But mostly, I remember the compassion and love I felt in her presence. I can still see the twinkle in her eye as she gently put her arm around me and smiled. I felt safe in those loving arms.

My sixth grade teacher entered my essay in a Modern Woodman of America contest, and I won. The trophy was nothing compared to the excitement I felt when I read my paper in front of the whole school. Having the courage to share my writing and feeling validated by adults in my community built confidence in my written words. Writing became a tool I have continued to use for healing over and over again in my life.

My mother was very busy as a homemaker and a full-time x-ray technician, but she still took time to volunteer at church. In the fall, we would gather pine cones to make wreaths, which she donated to the church auction. She also made golden loaves of bread, gooey caramel cinnamon rolls, and beautiful braids of sweet breads dotted with cherries. Her love has always been shown through baking, a trait she learned from her own mother. It is something I inherited and now share with my own girls. My mother's service to others was rooted in her daily prayer. She got up at five o'clock every morning to have quiet God time. I believe it was her way of remaining sane with three children and full-time work outside the house.

❦

The old coke machine with 10-cent bottles and the power car washer were great ways to entice my brothers and me to visit Dad's work. I would sit with a frosty bottle and watch the inner workings of an auto sales lot. It was impressive to see my dad in his element—talking, laughing, encouraging, helping someone buy the right car. Dad was well-respected, not at all like the typical slick used car salesman one might associate with this line of work. He treated others fairly and with honesty. I remember once when I was in high school, Dad came home and said he had quit his job. The company was not treating a customer right, and his belief in taking care of people was more important than the money he was making. It was an amazing lesson in integrity that I have carried through my life. My dad made friends everywhere he went. A quick stroll through the mall could actually take an hour because Dad frequently ran into someone he knew and would stop to talk.

Going to church was a family ritual on Sunday mornings. After mass, we would pick up my grandmother and bring her to our house for a day of baking and game playing. It didn't matter if it was Scrabble, King's Corners, 99 or 31, Grandma loved to play games, and she had great game-playing strategies. Although she was not a religious person, her kindness and acceptance of life was a part of who she was. Her love poured out in every cookie she made, in every game she played. The love of family and spending time together was an anchor in my life.

I had a pleasant childhood, surrounded by people who loved me. It didn't matter who was acting on my behalf, whether it was St. Blase or Grandma, a teacher or an angel like Sister Ann, faith was growing inside me. It helped me to believe in something much bigger than myself. I was building a belief in things felt but not seen.

Mom's Journal

Sunday, February 5th, Day 6

Jan's oxygen level was at 100%. It is not good for the lungs if it stays that high. She is still very swollen. Kidneys are not working well—the doctors are considering dialysis.

A Nurse's Perspective
Brenda Foster, ICU Nurse

The first weekend I took care of Jan, she had 15 lines and drains, eight IV pumps. Her weight was up 60 pounds to over 200. Someone handed me a picture and said, "This is Jan. This is who we want back." Since Jan was heavily sedated and unconscious, we did not know her as a person. The picture gave her personhood. We put the picture on the pegboard in Jan's room, and getting her back became our goal.

The Mysterious Network of Prayer
Rita Mailander, Becca's Preschool Teacher

I had told my mother about Jan, the young mother with three daughters who was gravely ill. She was praying fervently for her and even mentioned Jan to her dental hygienist in Atlantic, Iowa. As she described the situation, a knowing look came over the hygienist's face. "That is my cousin you are talking about." There were prayer chains reaching across the country.

As a result of many days in the Intensive Care Unit, I suffered from ICU Psychosis. This is a condition that often affects people who have been in ICU for longer than five days. The constant beeps of the machines, the lights, dehydration and medications can cause less REM sleep, which can contribute to a feeling of anxiousness, paranoia, and even violence. People poking me and drawing blood at all hours of the day did nothing to calm my nerves. Moving in and out of consciousness in the hospital where I didn't belong led me to be anxious and wild-eyed. In my dreams, I ran to get away from the terror of my life. In reality my body was in battle internally against a massive infection, while the doctors and nurses were doing everything they could to fight for my life from the outside. The constant beeping of the machines created a sense of agitation, a buzzing in my ears I couldn't stop. I longed for peace and quiet that never seemed to come because of the nature of ICU.

Where Dreams Carry Me

Down stairs I run,
through underground corridors.
Across threshold, I burst
into psychedelic purple room,
world spinning like
a disco ball gleaming over dance floor.

Hide Jan.

No safety here.

Must run again!
Back up stairs into green park.
Long lurching shadows.
Buzzing streetlight
spinning through my brain,
like swarming bees at my ear.

Fly Jan,
Can you?

Down crowded alley,
vendors selling street food,
steam, clamor, rising.
People at hand to help
but something pursues me still.

I run.

In a hospital
strapped in bed.
Callous male nurse
needles me without care
again and again.
Intense pain sears through me.
Help!

Thoughts fly
from place to place,
brain searching for quiet.
Constant beeping
drives me insane.

No one
in any dream
can wake me.

Where's safe?
Where's quiet?
Oh God,
Help!

Tony's Journal,

February 5th

Rita from church said there were 100 people at the prayer service for Jan. People from every aspect of the parish and every age group were there. I think once again, God has led us to the right place and the right community. We are truly blessed.

The Prayer Service
Fr. Ken Koehler, pastor of Most Precious Blood Parish at the time

Tragedy can often bring together and bond a community, more than it ever has been before. When the seriousness of Jan's illness became more evident, there grew a deep awareness at Most Precious Blood Church that we as a whole community had to do something. The feeling of complete helplessness was overwhelming. Two factors made the case stronger: Everyone knew Tony as one of the staff and baby Sarah grabbed all of our hearts.

I never had seen any prayer service so large and so emotional. There were adults with their children spending an hour or more in prayer. People learned that their prayer could be effective. The assurance that God would hear our prayer and guide us through this ordeal was absolute. I have never witnessed such confidence before. This experience taught the parish they could gather and people would know God's presence in their prayer.

The Power of Prayer
Lori Costanzo, family friend

I had never met Jan Haas in person, but I knew of her. Early in January, my then 6-year-old daughter Kristin would constantly talk about her friend Becca who was with her in Room Four at the MPB child care center. One day when I picked up Kristin from child care, I asked her about the beautiful brunette she had been playing with. She looked at me, exasperated, and said, "Mom, that's Becca!"

She then told me that Becca's mom had a new baby and was now very sick. Because Jan was Becca's mom and part of our Most Precious Blood Church community, I was concerned. Even though I didn't really know her, it was unimaginable to me that a young mother of three could be deathly ill—I had a hard time wrapping my brain around it. Within a week, while at a school mass, a visibly shaken priest announced that he had just given last rites to Jan. As the congregation sat stunned, he asked that we all stand, raise our arms and send a blessing to Jan. While I had done this many times for many reasons and many people, this time the experience was different. As I raised my arm and bowed my head, I could actually feel something physical in that church: something electric— something POWERFUL. A sense of calmness and certainty— impossible to explain—came over me. It was as if somehow I knew that she would be okay, that the strength and power and prayers of our community had really made a difference, and that prayer can actually be physical. It was such a powerful experience—I actually get goose bumps every time I think or talk about it.

Tony's Journal,

February 6th

Today I took a break from the hospital. After staying the night in the hospital, I planned on taking the girls to school and the sitter, spending some time by myself, and picking them up after lunch. But Becca did not sleep well last night. My mom said she was up until about 3:30 a.m. When I came home, she was certainly not herself.

I am concerned about how both Hannah and Becca are dealing with the situation. I have told them that Jan (Mom) is sick, but neither of them mentions her or asks about her. I spoke with Dr. W and he said kids are just as capable of denial as adults. I will get some pictures of Jan for them.

Based on this, Dorothy and I have decided not to spend the night at the hospital. We are five minutes from Jan's room if something should happen. The girls need me at home.

Mom's Journal,
Monday, February 6th, Day 7

Dr. G was in and said Jan is looking much better. He even said, "She is going to get out of here," and for him, that is saying a lot. Dr. O agrees that there is steady improvement. She has fluid in her lungs being drained by a chest tube, as well as fluid outside her lungs. The extra fluid presses on Jan's lungs, making it hard for her to breathe. A neurologist was in—checked for responses. Slow responses are to be expected with all the drug sedation and also with toxins not being cleared out by her kidneys. Dr. B, the surgeon, was also in and said she looks better. They will "mature" her ileostomy so it will produce waste products. The fever may indicate an infection or abscess somewhere, but they would have to do a CT scan to find it and that would be difficult at this point. Jan looks a little more like her own self, and has lost some of the swelling in her face.

It was very difficult for me to walk out of there Monday night, knowing none of us would be there with Jan. I just had to put my trust and faith in God...again!!

A Crack in the Rose Colored Glasses

EVEN A GOOD CHILDHOOD CONTAINS EXPERIENCES THAT aren't perfect. My perspective on seemingly innocent acts became limiting beliefs that colored my world.

In some ways, God took the form of the pastor of our church, the monsignor with salt and pepper hair who watched over his flock just as Jesus did in the bible stories. His black flowing robes with red buttons and trim enamored me. I remember him asking me if I did well on my report card. When I nodded yes, he dove into his pocket and produced a shiny quarter, as if he were a magician pulling a rabbit out of his hat.

This happened on several occasions, and I began to learn the importance of doing good to get a reward. I wonder how many quarters he put into his pocket every morning and how many children were awestruck by his presence. Maybe God was someone who rewarded me for good behavior. I looked at my dad in this same way— as long as I did things right, I was loved. Dad carried work and financial stress all day long and sometimes it exploded over all of us, especially if the house was a mess when he got home from work. I developed a fear of messing up, of not being good enough.

Being good enough meant doing the right things. I built a belief that just BEING was not good enough. As giving as my mother was, I didn't notice that she never took time for self-care. She was always doing—baking, cooking, cleaning, working, or volunteering. As the oldest of 11 children, my mother never had a childhood, a chance to play and be a kid. She was a responsible mother figure to her siblings. Thus, I never saw her without work in her hands, even if it was just a craft project in front of the television. I began to associate the act of doing with one's worth, and I learned to DO things to feel important.

Something I could DO was stay out of trouble. I am a product of all the benefits and the curses of Catholic school. One big curse was corporal punishment. In fourth grade, our whole class sat on their hands for 15 minutes, even though I can't imagine what we did to annoy the teacher so much. In fifth grade, one boy in particular had a regular date with trouble. I wonder how he is now, coping with the humiliation of being whacked on the behind in front of the class every week. His own embarrassment shaded my face pink.

I carried fear of failure as a stress that, at times, spewed out of me in rants toward my mother. In my teen years, we fought most of the time. Back then, I thought I just wanted to make different choices than my mother to show my independence. While that is partially true, the bigger truth is she was an easy target, a way to relieve the stress of trying to be perfect. My journals also bore the brunt of my anger and sadness, filled with poems about feeling alone and helpless, as if I hadn't a friend in the world.

So Perfectionism became my friend. She helped me get straight As and become a high school valedictorian. A 'B' on any assignment brought me to my knees, so I worked hard and proved myself worthy of love through my grades. What I didn't know at the time was that Perfectionism was friends with Judgment, and when they hung out together I found myself in a cycle of never being good enough. On the surface, I looked fine. I had friends, played sports and was involved in school activities. Yet, I judged myself harshly, and that often translated into judging others. I was an enemy with my own body. I found myself wanting on many occasions, never measuring up to the person I thought I should be. The self-confidence and self-trust I felt as a young child eroded away.

Mom's Journal,

Tuesday, February 7th, Day 8

Today turned out to be a good day for Jan. Her kidneys started functioning again and she lost 20-25 lbs., back down to 140. In the evening, Dr. W said she had made major improvements. She is off many medications and is beginning to look like Jan. They moved her to the suite on the floor, a room with an anteroom for family so we would be more comfortable. Her room is larger also. It took all seven of the nurses on the floor to move her. I felt quite optimistic when I left because it had been such a good day.

Mom's Journal,
Wednesday, February 8th, Day 9

This morning I met Dr. W coming into the hospital at the same time I did. He said Jan had a bad night. When we left, Jan had been spitting up a little green fluid from her mouth. Apparently, during the night she vomited, the respirator tube came out, and she aspirated, which is going to set her back. Dr. G was in and said she was out of the acute stage and into the secondary infection stage. We asked him if he still considered Jan "critical." He said he never answers that question. But he did say, "She's in ICU and has six specialists. What do you think?" By the time we left at 7:00 p.m., she was trying to blink her eyes in response to questions.

Meeting Tony

I WAS A SOPHOMORE AT COLORADO STATE UNIVERSITY AND met Tony, a junior, at John XXIII Parish in Fort Collins. Every Tuesday night, college students gathered for a soup supper and fellowship. Tony played his guitar for mass, and I fell in love with his singing voice. I liked the way he moved across the room, cowboy hat and boots, but was especially enamored with the gorgeous smile that peeked out behind a slim mustache gracing his lip. His sense of humor was evident when, for Halloween, Tony and his roommate dressed up as The Blues Brothers, and he didn't even mind when a silly dressed up clown— me—gave him a hug along with a splotch of white face paint on his black jacket.

Our first date in February was at The Junction, a local college hangout made popular by their plate-size chocolate chip cookies topped with a large scoop of cinnamon ice cream. I loved the way Tony's green eyes danced in the low light of evening, inviting me into his life with ease. Over spoonfuls of dessert, my heart dove deeper into Tony's captivating eyes. No wonder less than a month later, I knew Tony was the man I was going to marry.

We soon became inseparable. Notes and poems left on windshields and bike racks kept us connected across campus. I have to say love did nothing for my grades that semester. We often found ourselves on the campus lawn soaking up the sun and reading my English assignment, *Huckleberry Finn*, aloud to each other. The irony was that my English class was meeting while I played hooky.

In the summers of our college years, Tony lived in Boulder and worked for a special needs day camp in Lakewood. I worked as a waitress in Fort Collins. The long weeks apart were sprinkled with long phone calls and scattered letters. We lived for the weekends when we could connect and fall into rhythm with each other. Though our summers were challenging, they confirmed for both of us that we would make a life together. About a year after our first date, we were engaged to be married.

Tony was just beginning to look for places to study for a master's degree in theology, but already his studying led him to pick out the right readings for our wedding day. He wanted the readings to reflect the covenant we were making with each other and with God. Our wedding booklet read, "A chord of three strands is not easily broken." (Ecclesiastes 4:12) We were starting our married life together with God as the connecting force between us.

The Lines of Communication
Tracy Geygan, family friend

When Jan got sick, we had not yet become friends. We had met briefly a few months before, so I knew who she was, and I knew of her husband, Tony, because of his role with music at MPB. But our friendship and connection had not yet happened.

My oldest daughter was in the 3rd grade at MPB at the time, and she first came home with the news that Jan had gone back into the hospital a few days after the birth of her baby. During school announcements students had been asked to pray for Jan and the Haas family. And so the alert had been sounded, and immediately I was drawn to others who might have more information.

I think of the commercial for cell phone coverage, where they drop a pin on the map of the United States, and the lines spread out to fill in every city and town. In my mind that's how the news about Jan's illness traveled through the MPB community and beyond. With each wave of information, news spread from one person to another, each of us reaching out to others and to Jan and her family, sharing in the pain of Jan's fight in the tiny ways we could. To me, it felt like it was a medical race to get ahead of the infection, and the whole school and church community stood alert, praying from the sidelines as we watched the battle unfold. I prayed for Jan in my car, in bed at night, my girls and I prayed as a family after dinner, and the community joined in prayer. I reached outside my comfort zone to talk with other families, and as we shared the latest developments, new bonds were forged and reinforced. Together we despaired and together we rejoiced. I became more connected to the MPB community through prayer for Jan's healing.

Prayers from Far Away
In one of the many cards I received while in the hospital

"St. Pius (our parish in Cedar Rapids) continues to think of and pray for you. We sat by a couple in church this morning who asked how Jan is doing. They closed by saying, "Say hello for us. Well, don't bother. Tony and Jan probably wouldn't know us." I have to confess I didn't know their names either, but you are definitely in the prayers of people here."

Tony's Journal,
February 8th

Julie from Jan's work came today and dropped off three cases of formula, four packs of diapers, three packs of pull-ups and some stuffed bears for the girls. They also sponsored a blood drive to replace all the blood Jan used. They have had 40 people sign up already.

The church's business administrator offered to forgive our child care expenses at the early learning center for a few months. I thought it was generous and sensitive. Wonders never cease!

The generosity of people has been wonderful. People from all over have been very compassionate, generous and loving. This situation strikes amazingly close to home for most everyone. We have truly become icons of family tragedy and suffering for people around us. They have become for me, miracles, and a sign of God's loving presence.

I spoke with Becca today about whether she misses mom. She said, "No, she is only two blocks away!"

Mom's Journal,

Thursday, February 9th, Day 10

Jan's doctors feel she has more lung infection from the aspiration. She has a sore spot on the back of her head that is draining a little. No more vomiting today. The big battle today is her temperature that got up to almost 105. Twice during the day, they have iced down Jan—ice bags under her arms and ice water and cool cloths bathing her. She hates it, keeps shaking her head, "No!" Dr. G says a person's body temperature can actually go as high as 107 and not cause too much damage, but who wants to test that theory? Her body is fighting back, thank goodness!

Family Support
Aunt Judy Hahn, sister-in-law, married to one of Dorothy's four brothers. Dorothy also has six sisters who were great prayer warriors.

Norma, Debbie, Midge and I were in the kitchen emptying boxes because Dan and I had just moved into a new home. Norma got a phone call telling us about Jan. Right then and there, we kneeled on the kitchen floor and began to pray; we were all so worried but knew that if we put Jan in God's hands, He would know what to do. Another time later on, I asked for monetary contributions from the family for Jan and Tony and I received way more than expected. We have done that several times since then for others in the family, but Jan and Tony were the first recipients. It was then that I realized you can never ask too much from family.

Mom's Journal,

Friday, February 10th, Day 11

Jan has pneumonia and the doctors may try a CT scan to check for abscesses. There is always a risk in moving someone in such critical condition, but they feel the total body scan is necessary. They will also look at her head. One of their concerns is whether she could have had a stroke or other brain damage—any kind of bleed—because they are not getting much reaction from her.

Mom's Journal,
Saturday, February 11th, Day 12

The cat scan was negative, but Jan is worse. She had a bad night, and the doctors feel the infection is raging. She has some loss of kidney function and is getting quite jaundiced.

Mothers and Daughters

Pink cartoon characters
pop off the blue gown
eight-year-old Sarah wears.
Her slight smile cannot hide
the fear behind her brown eyes.

She awaits surgery,
not for removal of tonsils
or the setting of a broken bone,
but for the cracking open of skin and ribs
to stitch a congenital hole in her heart.

My arms provide little comfort
as she buries her head in my chest.
Tears form in my eyes,
and the weight
of motherhood bears down on me.

"One of the top ten surgeons in the world,"
I say to myself.
As they wheel Sarah away, the
"I can do this with my eyes closed"
confidence of the doctor
eases the fear in my heart.

Waiting.
Four hours of waiting.

And in a moment of lucidity,
I am taken back in time to
the scene of my own mother
sitting beside my sick bed,
in the same awful act of letting go.

For her,
there was no surgeon sharing bold confidence,
no historical outcome to prove good.

She was a woman,
praying her daughter might grab onto
a reason to live.
Praying God would bring peace.

And in that moment,
I am swirling in the protective love
of my mother
while sending that same love

out to my own daughter.

A kinship,
an understanding
of the long arduous journey of motherhood,
sweeps over me.
A prayer of gratitude
courses through my body.

I cry new tears
for life
for love
for mothers and daughters.

Daughters and mothers,
connected across time and space,
caught up in the mysterious pull
of umbilical love.

Mom's Journal,
Sunday, February 12th, Day 13

The nurse cut back on Jan's sedation. She is much more jaundiced today, but that is reversible. There is such a balancing act between what is good for one organ and not so good for another.

Little Improvements
Mary Gesing, family friend, as written in my bedside journal

Jan, I am sitting here on an early Sunday morning. It seems so peaceful being here with you. You had a restful night and appear to be comfortable now. I am so happy with the tiny, tiny improvements you have made since Thursday when I arrived. Each little improvement is a step in the right direction. Keep fighting! I hope you can feel the love that is surrounding you here. I am cherishing every moment before I have to go back to Cedar Rapids. You just rest and let your body fight this thing. I am beside you through it all and am keeping constant prayers.

Fight, Jan!
Aunt Doris (Doris Hug), as written in my bedside journal

Jan, we love you and pray for you constantly. We know the infection is still raging inside you and pray with all our hearts that you will put up a fight like we've never seen. We know you can do it!

Not Done with Jan
Sue Berscheid, family friend

I had a really hard time when Jan first got sick. I had a lot of battles with God, trying to come to peace with God's will for Jan. My feelings were compounded by the overwhelming joy and emotions of having my own newborn and thinking about Sarah. One day while I was ironing, tears were pouring down my face as I was thinking about Jan. Finally, I had to stop and say, "God, I'm not done with Jan yet and I don't want you to take her. But if you are going to take her, take her now." That very night, Jan started getting better.

A Special Gift
From Tyler, a young boy from the school

Dear Tony and Jan, My birthday is on February 12th. Instead of getting toys, I asked my friends to bring money for your family. I hope this money will help pay some hospital bills, and I hope Jan gets better.

Mom's Journal,
Monday, February 13th, Day 14

The night nurse says Jan has moved all extremities and has good strength in them, which is good news because that was a real concern. Her kidneys are doing better. The medication, Versed, which has kept Jan in a coma, is starting to wear off. She needs rest. Dr. O, the pulmonologist, was here and is pleased with her progress. She is doing some soundless coughing but that is good for her. The Group A Strep is gone—now they are treating the pneumonia and fungus.

This first day of no sedation was difficult for Jan. She has a nasogastric tube in her nose that runs down her throat as well as the ventilator tube in her mouth. She made lots of funny faces, trying to talk around the tubes. I wondered what she wanted to say. She looked so afraid—wrinkled brow, eyes wild and open. I think she knows who we are, but is so disoriented. We just continue to reassure her.

Tony's Journal,
February 14th, Day 15

I need to have a serious talk with Dorothy tomorrow. Though I appreciate her presence at the hospital, I am becoming concerned. I do not see her doing anything for herself. She has told many people that we need to be ready at any time to give up Jan. Everyone has followed her advice except her. She is totally engrossed in Jan's recovery. I think I will lay down the law with her—asking that she only be at the hospital in the mornings and dedicate the afternoons to something else. She has been returning to the hospital at night, eating by herself, and this is not healthy either. She needs to spend time doing things for herself. I hope I can present this to her so she doesn't get angry.

Tony

Where did he come from,
the one who calls to me?
Through frenzied sleep,
I cling to the sweet sound of his voice.

This man who,
in the heart of so much pain,
has the ability to see needs
others don't even know they have.

It is the same man,
my life companion,
who liberates me from
the legacy of my own mother.

In order to take care of others,
you must secure your own
oxygen mask first.

Mom's Journal,
Tuesday, February 14th, Day 15

All doctors say Jan is improving and hasn't gone backward for a few days. The doctors are concerned about a leak in her abdomen from somewhere, probably from the small bowel, but they aren't going to do anything about it yet. They would like to wait and do all the surgery at once, hopefully when she gets off the ventilator. Her metabolism needs are too great to wean her just yet. I haven't been in by Jan's bedside very much at all. They have been working on her constantly. Her temp is close to 103, and they have been using ice bags and just now changed to the cooling blanket, which she does not like!

Bound

I am running,
chased by an enemy
who hides in the dark.
He breathes down my neck.
I cannot catch my breath.

In a frenzy,
tossing and turning,
fighting the air,
I pull at tubes
to break free.

Alarms sound,
bringing the charges
who create order.

And then,

hands are bound,
tied to my bed,
suddenly paralyzed to

protect my own self.
Yet the enemy still lurks.
Only now I am trapped,
helpless,
a caged animal,
a stranger in my own crawling skin.

Even the drugged stupor
can't stop
FEAR
from swallowing me.

Mom's Journal,
Wednesday, February 15th, Day 16

The doctors plan to do an exploratory surgery to find the leak in her abdomen, at which time they will also do a tracheotomy. That will allow them to take the tube out of Jan's throat, stick it directly through her windpipe, and get some of the tape off her face. Her cheeks, lips and nose are sore and irritated. They say that a tracheotomy is much easier on a patient. I sure hope so. She still won't be able to talk. Maybe I will learn to lip read.

Dr. G finally admitted that he thinks Jan will survive. Since he always seemed like the eternal pessimist, his statement really means something. He calls the surgery a "minor setback."

❧

Jan made it over another hurdle. She is beginning to look like Jan now that she has a tracheotomy. The surgeons closed two openings where the tubes from the stomach and small bowel were. Usually, the skin and tissues heal up around these tubes, but because of the infection, there was no healing and one tube from the small bowel actually slipped out. Bowel content was seeping into the abdominal cavity causing infection. The surgeon flushed out the cavity with an antibiotic solution and then partially sewed up the abdomen, at least the innermost layers. The skin will come together and heal over. She will have a slight hernia at the top of the incision, and they will fix that later when she has surgery to reconnect the bowel.

It is hard watching Jan struggle with coming out of her sedation, trying to figure out what is happening to her. Her eyes get real wide, and she keeps looking around as if questioning everything. I hope this period doesn't last too long. Tony said she did sleep a little this afternoon.

Mom's Journal,
Thursday, February 16th, Day 17

The doctors say all things seem to be improving. We didn't lose any ground with the surgery yesterday, which is a plus. Jan still has a temperature of 102 degrees and her heart is working hard, beating 150 beats per minute. If she is improving, it is so slow as to not even be noticeable.

Mom's Journal,
Friday, February 17th, Day 18

I have the feeling that Jan might be angry at me, and I guess that is understandable. Striking out at those you love happens. Sometimes she turns her head away from me as though saying, "I don't want to see you!" Once, when I told her I was going to make phone calls—that Dad would be coming to see her tomorrow—she smiled. I'm sure she is frustrated because she can't speak and tell us what she is thinking.

She tries to mouth words but we can't seem to make them out.

Jan is down to four tubes or lines—two IV lines, the NG tube into her stomach and the respirator. The first two weeks, Jan had two nurses around the clock who started at the top and changed all the tubes and drains, and by the time they got to the bottom, they took vital signs, made sure she was comfortable, and then started again. Two nurses 24 hours a day!

The nurses all call her their "miracle baby," because she has overcome so many obstacles. She is very weak, but they are astonished at how responsive she is.

Worthy of Love

IT IS AMAZING WHAT BEAUTIFUL LOVE CAN DO FOR THE soul. The energy of new love, of someone accepting you for who you are, with all your faults, is life-changing. Reflecting back on my childhood, I know my parents loved me and wanted the best for me. But it took someone new to point out what years of self-doubt had covered up. I have no doubt that Tony was meant to be my partner on this long journey of life. He helped me recognize my own self-worth. When we were first married, he suggested I put notes on the bathroom mirror that read, "You are beautiful and worthy of love." Repeating these statements daily was difficult at first, until the affirmations began to sink in and fill my well of self-confidence. I began a journey toward accepting myself as I am. There is a reason we are called human beings, not human doings.

With increased self-acceptance, I started loving myself more. That led to treating others with greater kindness and with less expectation and judgment.

After Tony's graduation from CSU, we moved to Minnesota so Tony could earn his master's degree in theology from St. John's University. I finished my bachelor's in elementary education at the College of St. Benedict, the women's college that works in partnership with St. Johns. We lived in graduate student housing at SJU, the only married couple on campus. We made new friends with classmates, seminarians, and especially our floor mates on the third floor of Frank House. Often, we would pull the tables out into the middle of the landing and celebrate meals together, cooked in our tiny kitchen. We celebrated birthdays and Canadian Thanksgiving, and eventually, our small tables were filled with the voices and laughter of many wonderful friends.

The rhythm of St. Benedict permeated our lives, although we didn't fully understand it at the time. We enjoyed the balance between work and play, studying and walking in the woods, Uno with friends, and backgammon over dinner. We formed a small community that met in the mornings to pray, exposing us to various ways of talking to God. The long winter months helped us appreciate the act of slowing down and being in the space of reflection. The beauty of the woods and the soft falling snow surrounded us in a blanket of silence that began to take root. This silence and reflection would become an integral part of our healing journey in the future.

One month, as our funds ran low and our work study jobs wouldn't pay until the end of the week, we were discussing what to do when we heard a knock at the door. After climbing all the steps to the third floor, one of Tony's professors, an 83-year-old monk, handed over a full jar of watercress soup he had made after picking watercress all morning in the woods. Without knowing it, we were living in the moment, accepting God's grace as it came in the form of a sunny warm day, a walk at sunset, or a container of watercress soup. We have reflected back on this event many times in our married life. I believe our time at St. John's taught us to find God in the ordinary moments of our lives.

> *Fran Haas, Tony's mom, as written in the journal by my bedside*
>
> When I arrived this morning, Jan smiled in recognition. She is much more aware of us, and her moving lips show she is trying to communicate. But the frustration for both of us is that she can make no sound. There are pictures of Tony and the girls by her bed and a red rose taped to the bed rail. She has spent considerable time looking at these. I taped a picture of Sarah up after showing it to her, and I felt sure she knew Sarah. It took me awhile to figure out she wanted some of those pink sponges on a stick to moisten her mouth. After a few of these, she actually fell asleep!

Mom's Journal,

Saturday, February 18th, Day 19

We are working on exercising Jan's lungs to build up her strength. Physical therapy works with her a little bit now. Jan is holding her left arm up and moving it around and is moving her right arm a little bit.

She is not on any pain medication or sedation and hasn't been for about five days. She does not seem to be in pain. When they move her and it hurts, Jan makes a face and lets them know. They do give her a shot of morphine if they think she is in pain.

Mom's Journal,
Sunday, February 19th, Day 20

Up and down. As I've said before, I'm always apprehensive coming into the hospital for fear of what I'll find. Jan has some drainage from her incision, some infection coming from somewhere, probably the bowel, and she will have to go to surgery again. This is so difficult. More tears, hoping Jan does not notice how upset we are. I don't think she even recognizes us today. Yesterday, she was quite responsive and smiled a lot. By the time we left yesterday, she had been moving her left hand and holding it up. Today, she can barely lift her left hand up off the sheet.

The doctors started another broad spectrum antibiotic to take care of any intestinal bug in the abdomen but they will have to find out where the leak is coming from. We pray that it will not be a serious problem with the bowel.

We again must face the fact that Jan may not live through all of this. We don't know how much her body can take. Jan's nurse just came in and said, "She looks like she's fighting an infection, BUT she is fighting!! Her white blood count yesterday was 17,000. Today, it is 22,000.

❧

They came to get Jan at 2:30 p.m. and she was back in her room at 4:05 p.m., the surgeon trailing behind her. He only found one hole in her small bowel to stitch up, and then he cleaned out the abdominal cavity. There was quite a bit of pus and infection there. They didn't sew her up. They just put mesh over the open part of the abdomen and will now change the dressing every one or two days. He said the bowel looks good and is BEGINNING to heal. That's better than the report on Thursday when there was yet no sign of healing. Another hurdle! This is so hard to believe. It has been such a difficult day.

The Power of Mother Love

DEEP INSIDE, THE WELL OF LOVE THAT GREW FROM MY childhood and was refilled with Tony's attention and care sustained me. I was now drawing on the depth of this well in my time of need. How remarkable that the mysteriousness of love brought the very same priest who had blessed my throat as a young child, and who had performed our wedding ceremony, to my bedside to deliver last rights. He was now Tony's boss, the pastor at Most Precious Blood Church. God's ways were not for human understanding. Fighting death went beyond my own ability. My love of self was not strong enough to carry me through this challenge, and although I loved Tony dearly, I knew he could survive without me. But I didn't want to leave three little girls without a mother.

It was motherly, protective love for Becca, Hannah and Sarah that caused me to dig deep into my own being and pull out strength for life I never knew existed. They became my reason for surviving. This illness gave me a reason to believe in myself enough to know that my girls needed me, and I was going to do my best, even if it wasn't perfect, to get well and be their mother for a long time to come.

Mom's Journal,

Monday, February 20th, Day 21

Today is Jan's 31st birthday. Jan looks better today, smiled when I said good morning. White count is 22,000. Kidneys still look good. I stayed with Jan while the nurse changed Jan's dressings. The abdomen is open again, with a mesh dressing so the doctors can look inside. The muscle looks pink and healthy.

> **Happy Birthday**
> *Comment by Aunt Doris, as written in my bedside journal*
>
> Hi, Jan. This is not a great way to celebrate your birthday. I haven't seen you for a week, and I think you are looking much better. I even got a smile out of you today. Hang in there and keep fighting. We pray constantly for you and know that God is taking care of you. We love you!

Mom's Journal,

Tuesday, February 21st, Day 22

Jan looks good today, more rested and peaceful, not frantic. Her white count is down to 16,000, heart rate in the 130s, temp 101. The inside dressing was changed this morning and all looks OK. She slept some during the night. Dr. G said he is very pleased. Her lungs sound better than they ever have and show some signs of healing. Sounds like we are on our way again—upward!

Mom's Journal,

Wednesday, February 22nd, Day 23

Dr. K, one of the kidney specialists I hadn't met yet, was here and was also surprised and pleased at Jan's progress. Her kidney numbers are almost normal and the liver is getting better, yet she still has some yellow color to the white of her eyes. She is molting like a snake, losing the outer layer of skin. The thick callused areas on her hands and feet are shedding the most.

Mom's Journal,

Thursday, February 23rd, Day 24

Things seem to be status quo. The doctors are concerned about Jan's right knee. It is quite swollen and seems to be getting worse. Dr. O says things are relatively stable. They will try weaning her off the ventilator so she will be doing 10-15% of the breathing work. He said she is probably bleeding from the stomach. She had two more transfusions last night. They can't start tube feeding her until her bowels start to work.

Mom's Journal,

Friday, February 24th, Day 25

The surgery resident changed the inside wound packing today and said all looks good. He can see evidence of healing. Dr. P foresees leaving the abdomen open with a hernia, which will close by itself, and then we will hook the bowel back up in four to six months. That is what he says today. Tomorrow, that could all change.

Breathing Space

Who will tell whether one happy moment of love or the joy of breathing or walking on a bright morning and smelling the fresh air, is not worth all the suffering and effort which life implies.

Erich Fromm

Catching My Breath

LIVING IN COLORADO, IT IS NOT UNUSUAL TO HEAR AT least one story each year about someone being caught in an avalanche. I can only guess what that experience may be like, but I do know an avalanche is a good metaphor for the illness that caused me to go into a head-over-heels spin. I might equate the triggering of the avalanche to my doctor's visit early on that Tuesday morning, when I fainted. After that, everything was a blur. I was in the colossal slide, rolling down the steep incline of the mountain, snow roaring like thunder, crashing into trees, and gathering speed in its forward momentum. When the deafening roar finally stopped, I was disoriented and anxious, not knowing where I was. My dizziness dissipated, and thoughts began to form. "Am I dead? Wait. I must be alive. Why am I in this hospital? How did I get here? Am I hurt? Can I move?"

Questions tumbled out of my head. I was numb with shock over the immensity of this avalanche. The pain most pressing was the burning in my lungs as I tried to breathe. It was as if the weight of a mountain of snow lay upon my chest. I closed my eyes and allowed the drugs to surround me in an insulating cave of white snow. It would have been so easy to stay in that place and drift off to sleep. But another breath reminded me I was still alive and I had to fight. I imagined digging and clawing my way to the top of the snow drift, praying there was someone reaching for me on the other side.

Mom's Journal, Saturday,
February 26th, Day 26

They are weaning Jan from the respirator for a few times each day to build up her lungs, but it will still be weeks before she is off the ventilator. She had two one-hour periods off today and will have one more. She is learning to breathe again. Jan was able to communicate to us that she wanted a bath. She had a bath at 8:00 p.m. the night before, but her abdominal incision drained a lot and the bedding and dressings were saturated. After we were finished, she was very tired and went to sleep. God has answered the prayer for peace and rest. Jan doesn't have that scared, frightened look anymore, although she is frustrated when we can't figure out what she is trying to say.

Bathing

I am grateful for nighttime
when fluorescent lights are dimmed,
when the quiet moments
of being cared for
are louder than the beeps
of ICU machines.

My arm is held loosely
between the nurse's hip and elbow
while she wrings out a hot soapy towel.

Terry cloth runs over withered limbs,
massaging away dead skin,
exercising the muscles,
removing the staleness of
too many days in a bed.
The smell of clean
awakens my senses to the presence
of Marsha's gentle touch.

My arms and legs are scrubbed clean
as well as any other part
of my body that can be reached
amid bandages and bags.
Her small motions make
large shadows that dance on the walls—
arms, legs, and loving care move
in perfect rhythm.

After the bath,
sweet lavender
fills the air
as thick body cream
is lathered generously
over thirsty new skin,
covering me in luxury.

I am left in quiet for the night
while the scent of love

and a nurse's gentle touch
lingers behind,
smoothing the darkness of sleep.

Mom's Journal,
Sunday, February 26th, Day 27

Praise God! Jan had a good weekend, and all reports this morning from the doctors are good. Her metabolic needs are not as great, so they are adjusting the ventilator. The drainage from the abdominal cavity is slowly decreasing. Dr. B said there is probably another hole in the small bowel, but he thinks it will heal on its own without surgery. They won't start with a feeding tube until they are sure the hole is healed and the small bowel is working. Jan's right knee and elbow are causing her pain. Dr. W asked that the nurses set Jan up in a cardiac chair today. After being in a bed for so long, it is good for her to sit up. She has been in a special, very expensive hospital bed, $300 a day, which is in constant motion to prevent bed sores. She has a bald spot on the back of her head where she has lost most of her hair.

Mom's Journal
Monday, February 27th, Day 28

Jan is sleeping now. I have been working with her since I came in, trying to read her lips to figure out what she is saying. It is difficult with the breathing tube in her mouth, but we are getting better at communicating. Jan said "toothbrush," so we got her teeth brushed and that made her feel better. I asked her if she knew what happened to her and she said "No." I went through some of the story. She did remember fainting at the doctor's office but nothing after that. I told her how many people were praying for her, how many people loved her, about all the gifts and blood donors. It was pretty overwhelming. I showed her a picture of Sarah and asked if she remembers her—she doesn't—but I reassured her that it will all come back.

I rubbed her arms and legs again with lotion and peeled most of the dead skin off her feet. She said it didn't hurt. Jan said she wanted a blanket, so I covered her up and she went to sleep. She woke up momentarily and mouthed the words, "Don't leave without saying goodbye." I promised I wouldn't.

I WAS NUMB WITH THE EFFECTS OF VERSED, THE medication that kept me in a coma, away from the physical trauma my body experienced. As it began to wear off, I became more aware of the chaos around me, the aftermath of a serious slide. I knew something was wrong, because my whole body was out of sorts. Yet I was too caught up in the experience of living to care that I almost died. I wanted to know about the tubes coming out of every crevice of my body, why I struggled to breathe, and why so many machines were beeping in my ears. I was so worried about finding myself that when my mom showed me a picture of a little baby girl, I couldn't even begin to worry about who she was and how she was connected to me. Survival meant taking care of my own immediate needs, and there wasn't room to reflect on what was happening to those around me.

❧

I remember waking up from my drug-induced coma and seeing my mother, and I imagined we had this conversation:

"Mom, what are you doing here? What am I doing here?"

"Oh, Jan, I am so glad you are back! You have been very sick and in a coma for weeks. You have had six surgeries and have a long way to go before you are well." She proceeds to tell me the whole story of my illness.

"Where is Tony? Where are the girls?"

"Tony is at work and the girls are at school like usual."

"But why can't I be home? I am awake now. Can I please go home?"

This conversation never took place. I woke up in stages as my body slowly processed the last of the Versed. It was like walking through fog, trying to find my way back home. I also had a tube down my throat and was on a ventilator. Talking was painful, and it took time for me to learn how to communicate by using an alphabet board or relying on others to read my lips. The conversations happened over weeks, and little by little I learned what had happened to me. I didn't remember any of the surgeries, dying on the operating table, or bloating like a toad. I believe my body was still trying to shield me from the truth. Processing the trauma of my illness would take time.

Tony's Journal,
February 27, Day 28

Jan is doing better this week. We have been seven days without any surgery. With each day, we see more movement in her arms and legs and see her memory and cognitive abilities improve as well. It has been amazing to see the improvement between today and yesterday.

Jan knows where she is and that she has been in the hospital because of a massive infection. She does not know the extent of the surgeries, nor does she want to at this time.

Yesterday afternoon, the nurses changed some dressings and the ileostomy bag. I asked Jan if she knew what they were doing and she said, "No."

I asked if she wanted to know and she said "No" again. She can only take it in bits and pieces because of the intensity of this whole experience. We are letting her decide what she takes in and when.

We are entering the difficult part of Jan's recuperation. It will be challenging as Jan comes to terms with the violence that has been done to her body, the loss of significant body parts, and the loss of spending time with Sarah during the first part of her life. She is easily frustrated now with our inability to communicate. Sometimes I read her lips well; other times it is more difficult, and she gets upset. The speech therapist left an alphabet board in the room, so Jan can point and spell out words. I was having a hard time reading lips today, so Jan spelled out a word which I still could not figure out. Her fingers are quite atrophied and curved; it isn't obvious which letter she is pointing to. Jan said, "I'm so frustrated."

I replied, "I know you are frustrated. What are you frustrated about?"

She mouthed the words, "You can't spell!" I don't think she found the humor in the situation, but the nurse and I did.

Mom's Journal
Tuesday, February 28th, Day 29

    This experience is overwhelming for all of us. I've been remembering my own hysterectomy and how the "hot flashes" started within a short time after the surgery. Jan has been perspiring a lot. I asked Dr. W about it this morning to see if he thought she might be experiencing hot flashes—he hadn't thought of that. He ordered an estrogen patch to see if that helps.

Mom's Journal,
Wednesday, March 1, Day 30

    Jan looks good today—had a good night's sleep and slept part of the day. She seems to be dreaming a lot, because her arms are moving and she looks like she's talking to someone. She asked for her purse, her clothes, and her shoes. I told her the only personal thing here at the hospital is her glasses, which she has on. She seemed disappointed by this information.

    The speech therapist is working on getting a device to hook into the tracheotomy which would allow Jan to talk. That would be great!

    There were some tears today—Jan's and mine. She misses the girls and is tired of being in that bed. The GYN intern came in and introduced herself—said she helped with Jan's hysterectomy. Jan didn't know about that. This will only be the beginning of her grieving.

I am Woman

Swollen from the work
of pushing life into the world,
my uterus,
ravished with infection,
cut out and gone.
No more birthing daughters,
no sons.
How then am I a woman?

Where once a womb
nurtured cells and
grew my babies,
a void now exists.

Empty

Empty

Am I defined
by uterus or breasts,
body parts coded by DNA?

No!
I am woman!
I am so much more!
Giving life is my nature!

In the energetic womb of creativity,
thoughts, words, images
form and ripen.

My soul stretches with the elasticity
of uterine muscle,
nurturing, contracting,
giving space to that which needs to be born.

Some ideas slough off,
as natural as the monthly
rhythm my body still holds.

Others,
nurtured by attention
incubate and grow.

I labor to push them out into the world,
engrossed in the work of
wordsmithing ideas to birth.

In the final push,
a poem lies fresh on the page,
still covered in the messiness
of labor and delivery.
I mother it
and count its fingers and toes.
I marvel at its beauty.

I am woman.

Mom's Journal,

Thursday, March 2nd, Day 31

Jan got her hair washed, and I brushed it for her. I am sure the brush felt good on her scalp. A friend from church gave her the gift of a manicure, and I will give her a pedicure. Her feet are wrapped in warm towels and plastic now, and in a while, I will rub off some more old skin and paint her toenails. Tony said they had a good talk this afternoon. The physical therapist and speech therapist were here at the same time—had her sitting up, dangling her feet twice for 10 minutes each time. She wants to see baby Sarah, so Tony will bring her up on Saturday morning.

True Example of Faith and Trust
Colleen Deline, MPB community member

We all believed that Jan was getting the best care 24 hours a day at the hospital, so our concern turned towards Tony. Little did he realize what a profound impact he had on us! Here was this young father with two toddlers, a newborn, and a wife who was gravely ill. Tony would walk through the doors at church, and all eyes were on him. Everyone was watching and observing his words and actions during this horrible time in his life. Tony didn't have to say a word. He quietly moved forward each day, never drawing attention to himself. We never heard him complain or say, "Why me?" This humble man's faith was more visible than the shirt on his back. He was a true example of faith and trust.

Mom's Journal,
Friday, March 3rd, Day 32

At one time today, Jan and I were on the subject of God's plan for her life. She no longer has the option of giving birth. I told her I was grateful for her three beautiful girls. We put her entirely in God's hands during those first weeks in the hospital and had to learn to trust for the best. She said, "That must have been pretty scary for all of you." It truly was, but as I told her—God brought her back and He will make her well. The surgical resident who changed her inside dressing today told my friend Pat it could be months before the holes in her bowel close. I can't believe they won't try sewing them up rather than leaving them to drain for months!

Empty Space

Who am I?
A foreigner in a shell
of a body
I call home.
My anxious heart pounds
against skin that doesn't fit.

I wander passages
surrounded by gray,
searching for an inkling of light.

I cry out.
Hollow echoes return nothing.
I am alone.

The Loneliness.
Knowing that
the work
of healing
is mine to do
crushes me under darkness
I cannot escape.

On the walls of this prison
I scratch out my existence.
Why God? Why me?
I scream your name.

You call back to me;
The emptiness

swallows the sound
before it reaches me.

No answers to ease the pain.

Step, step,
one foot,
then the other,
pushing through numbness,
holding on to myself,
tasting paralyzing fear.

What if I can't find my way out?

Oh God,
What if I am not
stronger
than this despair
shackling me?

I push through.

Step, step,
hoping,
praying,
light is on the other side.

Mom's Journal,
Sunday, March 4th, Day 34

She can barely hold a pencil, but in childish, shaking handwriting, Jan wrote, "I should have a voice next week." She is looking forward to that. She sat up in the cardiac chair for almost an hour talking to Tony's sister, Mary Beth, and her husband, Jeff. When they eased her back into bed, she slept for four hours straight—a very good, quiet sleep, which she really needed.

Tony brought the girls up in the afternoon. There were some tears, but the visit did everyone good. Two-and-a-half-year-old Hannah sat on the stool by the side of the bed holding her mom's hand saying, "I love you, Mommy; I miss you, Mommy." I can't imagine what Jan was thinking. Five-and-a-half-year-old Becca talked for a few minutes and then sat in the chair and played by herself in the anteroom. She cried when they had to leave.

Fleeting Bliss

I see the janitor every day.
I hear his mop swish from side to side
under my bed.
Scrubbed from top to bottom,
stainless steel polished,
my room is spotless.

White

Sterile

Even in my medicated stupor
I can sense things are not right.

No windows to see color outside.
At least snow has more than one hue.

In an environment stark and antiseptic,

I toss and turn looking for home.

Where is my kitchen,
my books,
my husband?
Where are my children?
I miss the sound of their noise.

I scurry about in my dreams,
searching,
and all I see is white walls and sheets,
disinfected reminders
I am in a hospital
away from everyone I love.

Suddenly, a flash of color
crosses my line of sight.
A little red wagon
pulled by Tony
makes its way to my room,
complete with a baby girl in a pink bunny suit,
lying in front of
her two sisters, smaller to bigger,
wrapped in bright blue fleece coats.

Pure joy comes over me
and tears flow
as the girls hold my hand.

For a tiny second, I marvel
at their smiles,
their innocence.
Their love comforts me.

I am afraid for them
as my caravan of little loves,
travels back home,
a place I long to be.

The fingers of homesickness
wrap around my heart,
strangling the precious moment
of little girl love.

Color drains from my world again.

Mom's Journal,
Monday, March 6th, Day 35

Jan was smiling when I walked in—a good sign. They are weaning her from the respirator for more hours of each day. The physical therapist sat her on the edge of the bed, dangling her feet for seven minutes. Jan held herself up for some of that time. Then the nurses put her in the cardiac chair for close to 90 minutes. I exercised her legs for a while. She is definitely gaining strength in her right side. Jan must be getting better because she is beginning to complain and ask for things.

Mom's Journal,
Tuesday, March 7th, Day 36

Jan was despondent when I came in today. She said the nurse told her she may be out by Mother's Day, which is two months away, but she wants to be home NOW! Everyone tells her how good she is doing. Jan sees how far she has to progress to be well, while the rest of us can see how far she has already come.

Compounding Challenges

LOOKING BACK TO THOSE FIRST MONTHS IN THE HOSPITAL, I STILL can't imagine the upheaval my family experienced while I was in the middle of my own hell. Adjusting to the hospital routine, knowing I faced a long road to recovery must have taken its toll on my mom and my husband. My mother took a leave of absence from work, buoyed by sick days donated from her friends at the Colorado State University Health Center where she was an x-ray technician. Tony had a job, a sick wife, a mother-in-law who now lived with him, and the formidable undertaking of creating some sense of normalcy for three little girls. He lived moment to moment and didn't have time to think about anything else. Lucky for all of us, the community rallied around my family to provide formula, diapers, food, prayer, cleaning, and laundry. It was a force of worker bees bearing honey in the midst of pain.

I couldn't grasp all that the infection did to ravish my body. After so many weeks in a bed, I was very weak, and sitting up took immense energy. My only source of food at this time was TPN, total parenteral nutrition, which I received intravenously. Food was the last thing on my mind. The nasogastric tube snaking down my esophagus to my stomach went through my nose, making moving and talking uncomfortable.

I didn't have the luxury of time to grieve my

hysterectomy, although at a later date, I would reflect on losing a sense of womanhood. The loss of other body parts, like my gallbladder and a sizable amount of my intestine, paled in comparison to the immediate problems I faced every day. The calcification of my right knee, formed when the infection was coursing through my body, made walking painful. The idea of learning to breathe on my own again literally took my breath away! It was a daunting task.

I was still in shock over what was happening with my abdomen. Following six surgeries, I now had a ten-inch long by four-inch wide wound running from just under my ribcage down my center to my pubic bone. One might think of a wound as a cut with blood that needs to clot. But this was an opening in the abdominal wall left from prior surgeries, with granulated tissue, new connective tissue that forms during the healing process. It was complicated by an intestinal fistula, a hole the diameter of a pencil, formed at the top of the wound. Because intestinal tissue is so fragile, the doctors opted to let it heal on its own rather than try to repair it and rip more holes in my small bowel. As fluids moved through my digestive system they would pour out of the exposed fistula, filling the wound like a spring-fed lake, soaking many dressings a day. In the weeks and months to come, the caustic spring would leave my tender skin red, swollen, and in a constant state of irritation. The various wound bags and dressings that were used to contain the constant flow made me feel freakish and totally out of control with my body.

Above my right hip bone was the ileostomy stoma. The end of my small bowel had been brought through the abdominal wall forming the opening where waste would exit my body. The seal covering the stoma and an attachable bag caught all digestive waste that actually made it past the fistula. The end of my large intestine had been sewn to the inside of the abdominal wall so that when I had healed, my small and large intestines would be reconnected, and I could hopefully go back to normal bowel function.

With all of these complicated challenges, I didn't watch as nurses addressed issues with my abdomen. Shock and denial protected me from the whole truth about my situation.

I longed to be Jeannie from *I Dream of Jeannie*, the 1970s TV show, so I could blink my eyes and magically be in my rocking chair, cuddling my newborn Sarah. One wrinkle of the nose would make the hospital and all my health problems disappear. Yet another blink would find me on the couch at home, reading books to my girls.

But there was no magic here, no way to skip this hell. I had to walk through it. Eventually, I had to accept I was on a long, difficult road to recovery.

Mom's Journal,
Wednesday, March 8th, Day 37

Jan seems to be having another good day. The talking tracheotomy (a special device to help patients talk in a low whisper without losing ventilation) does not work well, but we are conversing a lot. The doctors are hoping to get Jan off the ventilator within a week.

Dr. G and Dr. W were here when I came. They are pleased—Dr. G is optimistic!! The pessimist is optimistic!

Mom's Journal,
Thursday, March 9th, Day 38

When I came in this morning, Jan said she didn't feel good. She was eating bites of a Popsicle. The emotions of the illness are catching up to her. She has a new nurse today. I could tell by how neat everything looked!

She gave Jan the shot she needs to lower stomach secretions in her thigh (3 times a day) and it really burned, so she found out it can be given intravenously. One less painful procedure to endure.

Dr. W ordered a larger dose estrogen patch that should help with the hot flashes. The surgery resident came in to change the inside dressing, so I asked if I could watch. I think he was a little reluctant, worried I might pass out. I reassured him. Actually, all I could see was a layer of granular tissues that has a great supply of blood vessels. There is pink muscle tissue around the edge of the wound. He showed me the hole. It is quite small. The resident said that the wound seems to be healing. Thank God!

Dr. O worked on the tracheotomy—trying to get Jan to talk. They fixed it differently than yesterday, and Jan could hear her voice. That made her happy. It shouldn't be many more days until she is off the vent.

Mom's Journal,
Friday, March 10th, Day 39

Jan was up in the "Pink Cadillac," the cardiac chair, for three hours. She was also completely off the vent for 25 minutes and could talk.

I told Dr. W, Jan's gastroenterologist, that she would love a glass of ice cold water. He said, "I don't know why not," and called Dr. O, who gave his approval. There were four nurses plus Dr. W to see the heavenly expression on her face when she had that first drink after 39 days!

Satisfaction

Purple iris
opens up to heaven,
petals like tongues
catching the glistening drops
of morning dew.

Mist from a lawn sprinkler
is a refreshing pick-me-up in late afternoon.
The smell of summer's damp grass
lingers in my nose.

A surprise shower of raindrops
tumbles from a sunny evening sky.
Dirt turns dark brown,
absorbing moisture like
a puppy soaks in praise.

I am taken back in time
to my first taste of

water in 39 days.

My parched mouth,
dry as dust,
craves moisture
like petals of the iris.
As the nectar of life
pours down like rain,
I smell the coolness rising
and am captured by the moment
as my shriveled body
swells with kindness,
quenching a need deeper
than thirst.

I gulp satisfaction.

Mom's Journal, Saturday,
March 11th, Day 40

When I arrived today, Jan was doing physical therapy. She was in the midst of a four-hour wean, and as time wore on, she seemed to get quite tired. I washed and dried her hair, and she put on one of the gowns I brought for her. It wasn't fancy, but at least it wasn't blue!

Dr. B was in—told Jan how lucky she is to be on the road to recovery, since the mortality rate for this illness is so high. One in five people who contract invasive strep A will die. One-third of those with this disease will develop streptococcal toxic shock syndrome. As blood pressure drops, critical organs start to shut down. We were so lucky to have amazing doctors who knew what to do at the right time. Their quick thinking and decisiveness saved Jan's life.

Dr. M spent quite a bit of time talking with Jan. He will increase her patch strength to decrease the hot flashes. She also has a urinary tract infection, so they have to change her Foley catheter to one that can be irrigated. One more annoyance!

The doctors are also concerned about her knee, which is not improving, and they really don't know what is wrong with it. She had weird red markings on the lateral side of the knee. They seem more pronounced today.

Mom's Journal,
Monday, March 13th, Day 42

Today is another down, blue day. Jan was off the respirator for a total of 11 hours yesterday, and she was weaning when I came this morning. She is more tired—says it is harder to breathe. Brenda is her nurse today and is great at trying things to make her feel better. She shampooed Jan's hair, and I dried and tried to style it. Brenda brought some ice cream, and Jan had about one teaspoon. She didn't think it tasted all that great, and it may have contributed to her cough, so it went back to the freezer.

Dr. G gave her another IV antibiotic for the bladder infection and one to take care of the knee—if there is infection in it. We are still waiting for a neurology consult on the knee. The occupational therapist brought a jar of "Silly Putty" and an exercise band for Jan's arms and fingers. She is gaining some strength, even though she doesn't see it.

Gone Fishin'

Planning my escape
in my wheeled reclining chair.

Newfound freedom
from six weeks in a bed,
I learn to sit up,
stand and pivot
into the Pink Cadillac.

The work is long and unending,
One minute 'til I turn blue;
then ten, twenty,
at last sixty minutes
in an upright position.

Today the sun shines
and calls my name.
Flowers bloom.
I hear the fishin' is good.

Three nurses
load up the Cadillac—
a heart monitor,
IV Pole,
oxygen tank,
and ventilator.
Get me outside!

We leave a note
for Tony:

"Gone Fishin"
will point him
to my heart's solace.

Free! Free!
I soak in the sun,
the aria of birdsong
and sweet fragrance of daffodils.

I almost forget
the Pink Cadillac.

I close my eyes,
run through a field of flowers.
I am alive!

Spring will come for me too,
though this year,
I am a late bloomer.

Mom's Journal,

Tuesday, March 14th, Day 43

When I got here this morning, Jan was sleeping, because she didn't sleep much at all last night. Dr. M is concerned about the rapid heartbeat. Since she is not as sick now, it should be slowing down. He has heard a slight murmur at times and wants to have a cardiologist check it out.

A couple of days ago, Jan wrote, "I will journal about what a different world I'm living in. I feel very disconnected from the rest of the world." She wants a tape recorder to journal with, since she can't write well.

Mom's Journal,
Wednesday, March 15th, Day 44

The doctors took Jan off the vent, and she can talk to me in her own voice! It quickly zaps her energy. She got pretty agitated and told us she feels like she will never get off the vent because she gets so tired. We tried to explain to her that sometimes she needs to go back on the ventilator to rest.

Jan said she doesn't feel very close to God right now. She says she doesn't really feel anger, but is questioning "why." I reassured her that her feelings are normal. God is always there for her and loves her just the same. It distresses her that she has so much support, but she still has to do all the work—an insurmountable task.

Tony said the physical therapists had Jan stand up in a walker today. She didn't walk, but at least she knows she can stand.

A cardiologist had been in to check Jan. He thinks she will be fine. Her rapid heart beat, in the 120s, is just a reaction to being so sick. She is now getting medication to slow her heart rate.

Breathing

Dark night
under blinding fluorescent lights.
I pull a breath into my chest,
yet lungs barely move.

So far down,
in a deep well
struggling to get out.

Dying,
buried alive.
Earth's weight above me
flattens atrophied lungs.

Each tiny breath
pounds my heart.
I am living,
embraced by fiery hell.

Can't breathe!
Hook me back up!

My Fix

Attached to machine
like a child to breast.
Don't wean me!

Mom's Journal,
Thursday, March 16th, Day 45

Dr. R, a neurologist, ordered an MRI to see if there is any nerve damage, scar tissue, abscess, or other problem in the spine that might be causing compression on the nerves of Jan's leg. He also ordered a bone scan for her knee and ankle to check for arthritis, etc. They are trying to get those tests scheduled. Getting Jan to radiology will be a major undertaking, and the MRI could be claustrophobic for her.

Dr. O was here and didn't really examine Jan because she is sleeping a little now after a shot of valium. She did a lot of coughing last night—maybe slept four hours. Dr. O is concerned about pneumonia again—her chest x-ray was slightly hazy. Her cough does sound tight.

Respiratory therapy will loosen up the mucous in her chest.

Jan was telling me this morning that she remembers arguing with the nurses about oxygen masks when she first came to the hospital. She said she also had a dream about doctors and nurses working hard to save her. I told her that was no dream—IT WAS REAL!

I washed Jan's hair while the physical therapist worked on her legs. Then they sat her up on the edge of the Pink Cadillac for 10 minutes, and most of that time she held herself up. She seems to breathe better when she is working at something or has her mind on something else. Jan said it felt good to have upper body strength to sit up. She can't use her abdominal muscles because she has the open wound.

Mom's Journal,
Friday, March 17th, Day 46

Jan has been off the vent two days now. When she woke up from a nap, the nurse was summoned, and we all clapped as the ventilator was removed from Jan's room.

Susie, the nurse, also pulled out her nasogastric tube today. Another huge step! She can have sips of water but still no food.

The IV nurse tried repeatedly to put in a PICC line, a line in her arm that can stay for weeks, through which they can give IVs and take blood. Finally, she got it in her right arm. She has had a subclavian, or central line, which runs from the blood vessels above the heart, but central lines are too susceptible to infection. The position of the PICC line offers the same benefits, only at a further distance from the heart for less chance of infection. When the PICC line went in, the subclavian line came out. Dr. O changed the tracheotomy to a smaller one. After several more days, it will be out altogether!

Tony brought Sarah in for a visit—she was sleeping in the stroller.

Susie plans to get Jan in the Pink Cadillac to visit the second floor where Jan will be transferring.

The speech therapist gave Jan a memory test, such as repeating sequences of four, five and six numbers; short sentences, personal questions; such as age, months, days of the week, seasons, and holidays. Jan passed with flying colors.

We have to celebrate these seemingly small successes. Jan has such a long way to go to be well, but each day she is taking huge steps forward. Sometimes they are hard to see, but today, there were many visible milestones to be celebrated.

Mom's Journal,
Saturday, March 18th, Day 47

Although I have a lot to do today, I enjoyed being home in the quiet house, hearing the birds sing, appreciating spring, the budding plants...all the time thinking of Jan, remembering what Brenda said, that at least I get Saturdays off—Jan doesn't get any days off! The girls are with Meg, who works with Tony, enjoying their special day out at the zoo. I hope Tony is enjoying his time at a work conference in San Diego.

Saturdays with Becca, Hannah, Sarah and my Daughter Kate
Meg Meersman, family friend

Saturday was Tony's day to visit Jan in the hospital, to run errands and maybe squeeze in some time for himself (I hoped). This one day a week was a gift for me and my daughter Kate. In return, we gave the girls normal time without the stress of Mom being sick, Dad busy, grandparents worried. We created our own world.

Every Saturday, when the girls got into the car, I would ask, "What should we do today?" I looked in the rearview mirror and watched their eyes light up with possibilities.

"Let's play dress up! Let's go to the park. I want to see a movie. It's nice, so let's go to the zoo." The girls enjoyed the freedom of picking their own activities. With peanut butter and honey sandwiches in tow, we were on our way to adventures.

When it came time for naps, there were no complaints. All four girls climbed into my king-size bed, and Kate read aloud. Within minutes, all four of them would be asleep. This was my moment to peek in and reflect on my own blessings. Taking the time to grant little girls' wishes was easy. The love I got in return was infinite.

After nap time the giggles were abundant. "No laughing aloud!" I would jokingly boom. Silence was held for a second and then more laughter rang through the house.

Mom's Journal,
Sunday, March 19th, Day 48

Jan was not herself when Dad and I arrived today. She was quite warm and hadn't been cleaned up. They don't plan to cover the tracheotomy for talking today—talking wears Jan out. Dr. O's partner is suggesting she be on the vent for a night or two until she gets stronger. She hates the thought of it—feels like it's going backward, but she may need the rest. She will have a blood gas study late this afternoon, and then they will decide what to do.

Jan said she was in x-ray for two hours on her back on a hard table yesterday—didn't like it at all. The physical therapists had Jan stand for a short time, sit on the edge of the cardiac chair, and do exercises. They said she did well. I called about 8:30 p.m., and Jan's nurse said they would not put her back on the vent. They will see how she does during the night.

Mom's Journal,
Monday, March 20th, Day 49

Dr. G was in with the good news that there is no apparent bone infection—thank God! Dr. O talked to Jan for quite awhile about her breathing. Psychologically, she is anxious—feels she can't catch her breath. She needs to work on breathing slowly and deeply—much easier said than done. She has been working hard and struggles to relax.

On a daily basis, staff from the hospital stops by to see how Jan looks. The nurse said that visitors are pleased with her progress, because Jan was so close to NOT making it.

Time Perspective

EVERYWHERE I LOOK I SEE SHARP LINES AND ANGLES. I observe the way the door frame intersects the straight bar of the nurse's desk and the way tiles on the floor continue their straight path out of my line of sight. In front of the door frame is the outline of my bed, sometimes lower, sometimes higher, as I peer out of my room. Even the square-ness of the TV juts out from the nook where two walls touch. Nothing in this room creates warmth. Curtains hang in parallel strips, sterile. Stainless steel sinks and knobs give the place an industrial feel, complete with the constant hum of machines. Clearly, this is not the place for a healthy person.

The round clock with its slow-moving hands haunts me. The black arrows move like snails around the numbers, especially at night when the dark has settled and the beeping machines keep me awake. At ten o'clock, the square TV screen turns black at the touch of a finger, and the call button brings the nurse, who gives me something to induce rest. My eyelids get heavy, and I pray for sleep.

I am awakened by a crazy dream where I am waiting for my mother to take me home, but she doesn't have the right paperwork. Noisy, constant beeps bring me back to reality. Now, the darts point to the twelve and two. Shadows creep around my room in long tendrils that reach out and wrap me in tense isolation.

After restless hours of tossing and turning, the clock's two hands stand at attention, pointing to twelve and six, just like the IV pole that stands guard by my bed, a constant sentry, his waist girded with a machine that pumps not bullets but measures of drugs and nutrients that keep me alive. Time for the blood warriors to arrive—they carry supplies in plastic-handled tubs and work in near dark, causing me pain even when I am half asleep. Sharp needles poke deeply into my wrist, drawing blood gases from buried veins. Silent tears roll down my cheeks, the blood draw releasing pent-up emotions.

The clock sentry disappears and my heart quickens, waiting for the next triangle to appear on the clock, when the hands reach the eight and the six. At 8:30 a.m., my mother arrives. All the angles of my room suddenly move away, my breathing slows, and I soak in the love that surrounds me.

Finally, I notice the softness of the room—the way the pillows surround my bed, keeping my body propped up and comfortable. The nurse brushes my arm as she checks my IV. Pictures of the girls taped on the IV pole remind me of what I am fighting for. I love the tenderness of my mother's smile, which makes a tiny smile appear on my own face.

Why in these soft hours of daylight do the hands of the clock speed by like the hare in the race?

I am in a flurry of activity with physical therapy—moving from bed to chair and transferring back, talking with Mom, and napping when I feel safe in the presence of motherly love.

At 1:30 p.m., my mother leaves and Tony arrives for the afternoon. He is my guiding strength as I fight to regain my health. Often, when I am away at therapy or getting tests, he sleeps on my bed and tries to catch up from the long days that pull him in so many directions. We talk about the girls and work and try to pretend that our lives are perfectly normal.

When the black hands make it five o'clock, Tony leaves for the evening, and the darkness of late afternoon settles over me like a fog. The snail returns to run the race, the hare gone in a flash.

Eventually, there will be visitors at night. For now, I must be content with the company of TV and the chatter of nurses who have befriended me. The sharpness of my room closes back around me, and pointers on the clock inch their way through the night. I wait for the next morning when my heart will lighten once again. My mother will arrive—the love I have known all my life.

Mom's Journal,
Tuesday, March 21st, Day 50

This has not been one of Jan's better days. She slept until 4:00 a.m., and then the day took the best of her. At about 10:00 a.m., Rene gave her a shot of Sandostatin to slow down the drainage, and she experienced dizziness, heat, chest pain, and upper abdominal pain. Her face was flushed for a couple of hours afterward, and her temperature went up to 100 plus. Her heart rate has been in the 150s all day. They changed her dressings and put her up in the chair, but she had back and leg pain and was feeling so badly, she only stayed up for about 30 minutes and fell asleep.

Mom's Journal,
Wednesday, March 22nd, Day 51

Jan was resting when I came—worn out from another night of little sleep. The orthopedist thinks she has extra calcium deposits in the right knee, caused by the sloughing off of tissue when the infection was active. They may do a CAT scan of the knee when she has her abdominal CT.

Occupational therapy and speech therapy have been here, and physical therapy is here now. Jan stood on one foot for 50 seconds and then did 80 seconds the second time. Jan was seated in a plain chair and had to move from the bed to chair by pivoting on her left foot. In doing the exercise, she accidentally bent her knee, which caused her a great deal of pain. She stayed in the chair with ice on her knee for 90 minutes.

Jan asked me later if I thought we would ever know why this happened. I told her we probably wouldn't until we get to heaven. However, there may be some good to come out of her suffering.

It amazes me to see how involved the nurses have become, how much a miracle they see in survival and progress. The picture of Jan and Tony before the illness gave the medical staff a goal—to see her as healthy and glowing as she is in the picture. They have been so good to her.

Microwaved Blankets

My lips shiver in
dark despair
deep within.
I lie on the cold metal table
waiting for a CT scan.

I am away from my girls and Tony and
all the places I would rather be
than in this reality called
illness and hospital.
My teeth chatter as my jaw shakes.
The warm leaking fluid from
the ileostomy
freezes me.

Caring hands
of the nurse who never leaves
cannot thaw the winter,
the distance I feel from normal,
the separation from family,
my home.

Three hours later,
in my room,
cold darkness fades.
Layer upon layer of microwaved blankets
pink my skin,
thaw layers of frustration,
melt hours of pain.

My eyes close,
bringing me
my true home,
the loving embrace
of Mother God's arms.

My shivering stops.
I am at peace.

Mom's Journal,
Friday, March 24th, Day 53

Dr. G had a long talk with Jan this morning. He said he sees the sickest patients in the hospital, and she was the sickest he has seen in a long, long time. Dr. O was in—changed the tracheotomy site dressing to a much smaller one. She is still leaking air. She was able to talk him into less breathing treatments and one less medication, which is making her cough. Coughing tires her out and makes her ache all over. Talking is becoming easier for her.

I was able to see Jan's x-rays. The size of the calcification in her right knee amazes me. No wonder it hurts.

Jan gets discouraged but is able to pick herself back up. Physical therapy is tiring and hard, but she puts her heart into it.

Jan may be in the anger stage of grief. She knows it's a miracle she's alive, but doesn't feel the miracle, doesn't feel close to God. I told her to depend on others to pray for her.

Mom's Journal,
Saturday, March 25th, Day 54.

Jan took ten steps today!

Mom's Journal,
Sunday, March 26th, Day 55

Jan was in great spirits today when we got here, and loved the pretty robe we brought her. Keith was surprised at her progress. It has been so difficult for him to see his daughter in the hospital. For physical therapy today, she took steps to the chair and turned around and backed up, and she did the same maneuvers when she got back in bed. An air brace for her knee during transfers helps. Jan can bend her right knee to 40 degrees, a tremendous improvement from two weeks ago.

Dr. S ordered a liquid diet. She will even get a tray tonight! We will see if she puts out too much fluid. She is now getting Percocet for pain instead of morphine shots.

Tony took Hannah to see Jan about 2:30 p.m. and came home about 6:00 p.m. with the news that they were moving Jan out of ICU at 7:30 p.m. tonight. The move had been planned for two days from now, but ICU was filling up fast and they needed the space. We ate a quick dinner. Tony and Becca went to the grocery store, and then they dropped me off to be with Jan during the move and to stay the night. Jan was apprehensive and nervous; she was afraid she would be considered a "nuisance" in her new room and would bother the nurses too much.

I took pictures of the regular nurses with Jan—Pat, Donna,

Eileen, and Marsha. We hope to be able to get pictures of others later, especially Susie and Brenda. Jan shed a few tears at leaving her "home," and she got hugs from the nurses. They were short of help and busy in ICU, but that didn't stop Marsha from stopping in later in the evening to check on Jan. She said they rarely offer their assistance, but told Jan to call ICU if she had any problems.

Hannah said something quirky on her quick visit to Jan. She was busy polishing the stainless steel buttons in the ICU room when, out of the blue, she turned and looked at Jan and said, "Mom, get up!" As if all Jan needed to get well was an order from her young daughter!

> **From Grandma's Tales of Prince Charming and "Catch the Light"**
> *Carol Haas, Tony's stepmother*
>
> There's no denying Jan's illness was a nightmare, but it had some very positive bright spots: watching brave and valiant Tony, the patience and calmness of Jan's mom, the generosity of the friends at our church, and of course, the special times with the three girls. Fortunately, we were in the position to be able to help a lot with the girls. They had many "mothers" during that time. We were able to pick them up and sometimes take them to school and day care. We played many games in the car, which they still remember, such as "catch the light from the flashlight" and Cinderella. Of course, Grandpa was Prince Charming, and baby Sarah was a wicked stepsister. We sang silly songs from a children's tape and ate dinner together and often bathed them and put them to bed. It was a difficult situation, yet not many grandparents get such a special bonding time!

Breathing Space

Death no longer lurks in the shadows,
his moment thwarted
by a mysterious fabric
of prayer, love and competent care.

Shoulders drop from flight,
relax into here and now.
Sleep comes without nightmares,
and even tense moments are
searched for evidence of good.

Lungs fill tentatively
without machine,
learning now to
breathe life into every
cell of my being.

Caught in between,
I choose to walk
closer to the light,
determined to live wide awake
and not be counted
among the walking dead.

Becca's First Touch after a Long Absence

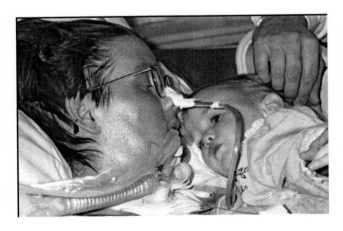

Hannah in My Arms

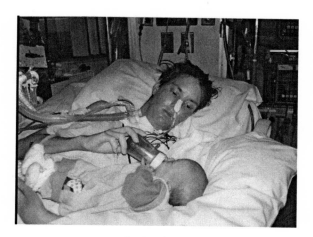

Feeding Sarah

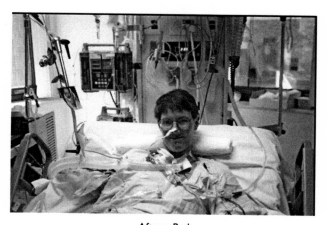

After a Bath

Transitions

It is in moments of illness that we are compelled to recognize that we live not alone but chained to a creature of a different kingdom, whole worlds apart, who has no knowledge of us and by whom it is impossible to make ourselves understood:
our body.

Marcel Proust

The Surgical Floor

Mom's Journal,
Monday, March 27th, Day 56

Today was Jan's first day in a regular room. My own rollaway bed left plenty to be desired, but Jan slept fairly well. It is more quiet here than in ICU. Jan's biggest problem is getting into a comfortable position. Her right leg has shooting pains off and on. When the physical therapist came, Jan walked about eight feet. She sees progress. It was a day of getting used to new surroundings.

Mom's Journal,
Tuesday, March 28th, Day 57

Not one of Jan's better days. When I came in, the nurse was working on her dressings. She has a rash around the incision and also a very red area around the ileostomy. The catheter was removed this morning because of infection. Physical therapy came and helped Jan practice getting off and on the commode. They got her a pair of net panties to help hold her dressings. She got up, sat on the commode, and was able to void almost immediately. What a huge accomplishment! Hopefully, she won't be catheterized again. Sarah spent the afternoon in Jan's room.

Sarah

Propped up
against foam blocks
where my feet rest,
baby Sarah stares at the overhead lights.

I whisper her name.
Brown eyes pierce me,
search me
the stranger,
for reasons she is here
in this strange place.

I stare back,
searching too
for signs of the daughter
to whom I gave birth
in a moment of light,
smothered now
in so much darkness.

I don't know her eyes,
her smile,
or recognize the grasp of little fingers around
mine
as she might nurse at breast.
All things a mother knows about her baby.

It will be years before
I know this child,
this girl who is more like me

than my other daughters.

&

At sixteen,
her gaze pierces me still,
asking questions
I cannot answer.

There are times
when she is a stranger in my house,
a girl whose mysterious moods
I don't understand.

Then I catch a glimpse of my own teenage self,
feisty, determined,
always needing to be right,
angry at traits shared with Mom.

It is a battle I fight with myself (Sarah),
searching for and finding me (us)
and losing myself (us) again.
Caught up in expectations
and always falling short.

We are magnets repelling,
pulling away,
searching for differences.
Yet in a split second,
our polarities align.
We are united,
rejoicing in our sameness.

Who is this girl—
my baby whose pull away from me

is so painful and necessary?
This young woman
whose light has always been
shining in the darkness,
waiting for me to open my eyes and see?

Mom's Journal,
Wednesday, March 29th, Day 58

Jan was determined to walk today, so the physical therapist, Jan, and the walker went to the doorway—about 18 feet—as far as the oxygen tubing would allow. She is moving herself in bed so much better, turning on her side and moving into a sitting position. It is amazing progress. She reminds me of the two-year-old syndrome, "I can do it myself."

The Bedpan

ONE OF THE BIGGEST ADJUSTMENTS I HAD TO MAKE ON the "non-intensive care" floor was less medical attention from the nurses. At no other time was this more crucial than when I had to go to the bathroom. One night, I turned on the light to signal my nurse. Ten minutes later, I was still waiting. In the hospital, the nurses don't look too kindly on you getting out of bed to use the toilet, especially if you are just out of ICU and still attached to machines on an IV pole. When you add a bum knee, a pair of crutches, and an open wound to the mix, it is an invitation for more disaster. A bedpan seemed like the right thing at the time. Finally, the haggard nurse arrived and helped me get situated as comfortably as I could on the cold bedpan. I then asked the question that changed my life in that moment.

I asked the nurse, "So, how many people on this floor do you have to adjust bedpans for?"

She looked me in the eye and said, "You are the only one." I was startled. Even today, as I run this conversation through my head, I can't guess whether or not she was telling the truth. Maybe I was the only one. It didn't seem possible since I was on a surgical floor and there were many people recovering from surgery. Maybe they all had catheters. But I felt truth in that statement for me, and something inside shifted. I knew that now was the time for me to step up and become more responsible for my own healing. It was time to help myself. No longer would I do what was most convenient, if you call a bedpan convenient. I vowed to push myself to the next level so I could get out of the hospital and be at home with my family. The very next night, with the nurse's help, I walked on crutches to and from the bathroom. I gained some self-respect.

Finding My Voice

Jan's Journal
Saturday, April 8th, Day 68

Good morning! I am speaking into a tape recorder for the first time, even though it has been in my possession for a week.

I do not feel like myself, away from the comforts of home and the people who ground me. I feel more like a lab animal with a grotesque wound that the scientists want to observe. Thoughts about illness tumble through my head and mix with the timid gratefulness I feel—it is difficult to sort out my feelings.

I am more aware of being alone since I left the ICU. Here, the nurses have more people to care for and less time to devote to one patient. A pivot out of bed and a walk to the bathroom can take 30 minutes or more, depending on how busy the nurses are. For someone who likes to be in control, this is frustrating.

Aside from waiting impatiently for help, I am making progress. Two days ago, I walked from my bed and across the hall, 20 to 25 feet. The nurse walked behind me with a wheelchair in case I got tired or my blood oxygen level got too high. The physical therapist held onto me with a strap wrapped tightly around my chest. When I walk with my crutches, it feels good to go somewhere!

Yesterday, for the first time in two-and-a-half months, I stood at the sink, brushed my teeth, and washed myself. Unbelievable! Becca thinks it is funny I am learning to do basic things. She loves the cones I stack for my eye-hand coordination. In many ways, I am a child again. At five-and-a-half, Becca is stronger than I am, weaving through the cones on the floor, skipping and laughing. She plays with the silly putty I use to strengthen my hands, rolling it into cookies, which she serves me. Her presence lightens the pressure in my lungs. I breathe in her hugs and kisses and feel much more at peace.

One-on-one visits from the girls have been great. It is easier for them to see me now that I don't have so many tubes. I look almost normal, except for the bandage on my neck where the breathing tube was and the fact that my hair is falling out. I miss holding two-and-a-half-year-old Hannah in my arms. I miss her sweet little voice and the way she scrunches her face when she is being silly. And I miss having favored parental status, knowing I was the one she called for—she always needed "Mama." Hannah is intimidated by all the tubes and machines. Now that I am looking better, I hope she feels more comfortable coming to visit me, even though holding her on my lap still isn't possible.

Sarah comes once a week. My poor little Sarah—I have not bonded with her yet. I only had four days with her before I got sick, and I was preoccupied—no quality time for getting lost in the love and joy of a new baby. I hope our relationship will develop over time.

In the hospital, all normal sense of time is lost. I know what day and time it is. I can look out the window and see that it is spring. Yet, I am stuck in a place that knows only one time, and that is shift rotation. Everything revolves around the changing of the guard. I yearn for the rhythm of my girls getting home from school, the sound of their laughter rather than the sound of beeping machines. I want family time—not medicine, physical therapy, and doctors and nurses analyzing my daily progress.

It is slow in coming, the realization that I am alive. I have moments of clarity when I realize the alternative to "this" is a headstone. Nurses hearten me by saying, "You know, you look better every day" and, "I am so glad you are here—you have a light inside you that touches others." I get choked up. I believe God is with me and somehow, through me, God's love is reaching other people.

I will spend some time at home on Easter. My plan is to be home for good on Mother's Day. I have five weeks to get in tip-top shape. It will take hard work, yet I know God is with me, and I draw strength from the prayers of the people around me. How strange to think that I have been in the hospital for two-and-a-half months! I really miss Tony, holding him, touching him, and hugging him. It is hard to be without him.

I guess I have been to hell and back, huh? Thank God I am back!

Tuesday, April 11th, Day 71

For physical therapy today, I walked 100 feet and then stood for five minutes. Because I am getting stronger, I need less oxygen and support. My left knee has a 40-degree bend in it, and Dr. O does not see much progress. He thinks surgery is necessary after I am nutritionally stable. I would rather have surgery before I leave the hospital than to wait, because I will want to drive. I think becoming mobile will help my overall recovery time.

The nurses have covered up the hole in my belly with a wound bag, one that connects to a suction catheter to pull out drainage. This allows me to cap the catheter and do physical therapy without the worry of leaking fluids. A catheter with a noisy machine feels like a step backwards, yet I think it will help the healing process.

Dr. P told me this morning I could have full liquids now, which means I can have puddings and cream soups. He also told me that a feeding tube is an option. If the fistula, or hole, is high enough in the intestine, we can use a feeding tube to plug the hole, which would eliminate my IVs. I would be fed twice a day through the feeding tube. I asked him how the hole would ever heal, and he said the intestine will form a tunnel around the tube, and when we pull the tube out the tunnel will close. This is an option to consider.

Tony came up with all the girls, but because my stomach hurt so much, I couldn't hold Sarah. I want to be "Mom" again, yet my role as a mom from a hospital bed is quite limited. Becca remembers that I am coming home this Sunday. She says, "Just for a little while Mom, until you're really ready to come home for good."

The tears make it hard to record my thoughts. I don't want to be over-emotional. My nurse Claudette said, "You want me to tell you why you are emotional?" She named off at least 20 reasons why I should be. She said, "Do not minimize what you have been through." I can cry, and it is perfectly normal.

Thursday, April 13th, Day 73

Dr. P already returned me to clear liquids because the thick liquids were leaving a residue on my wound that will hinder the healing process. Every step backward is depressing.

I told my physical therapist that when I walk, I want to keep moving. I do not want to slow down or back up, so I made sure that I walked at least 100 feet yesterday. Tomorrow will be at least 101 feet!

Friday, April 14th, Day 74

Today, I was taken to radiology at 7:00 a.m. for an upper GI test and was not helped until 8:30 a.m. A meeting we did not know about slowed all the testing. Five minutes after I drank the barium, I threw up. My anxiety level rose when the ileostomy bag started leaking. They brought me back to my room on a stretcher instead of a wheelchair. I was so worn out that I slept the rest of the morning.

In the afternoon, the ileostomy nurse took two-and-a-half hours to replace the wound bag and ileostomy bag. Tomorrow, they are going to stick a catheter in the fistula and use contrast to see where the hole is. This will let us know if a feeding tube is feasible. I am supposed to move to the rehabilitation floor next week.

Today, my friend Adele from church brought me two full bags of brand new dresses I can wear over t-shirts. It will be wonderful to get out of these hospital gowns. IV tubes and t-shirts don't often pair well, but my mom will figure something out. Her dresses wrap me in the tangible love of many people. Tonight, I walked 200 feet, all the way to the end of the hall and back! It was a great accomplishment.

A Healing Team
Brenda Foster, ICU Nurse

Jan's "team" was huge. The medical team was large, of course. It included so many disciplines: RNs, doctors, lab techs, radiology techs, PT, OT, wound nurse, pharmacy. Even the cleaning people knew who the young mom was because she was the talk of the hospital. It was a coordinated effort, and each person contributed to the outcome. Her team also included Jan's family who was spectacular in advocating for her. Jan's daughters kept her focused on the good.

Jan's journey would have been much more difficult, if not impossible, without the community team. How blessed this family was to have prayer chains and lots of volunteers who rose to the occasion to help.

Saturday, April 15th, Day 75

Tomorrow, I am spending some time at home. I'm excited and nervous at the same time. On the phone I told Becca, "There are a lot of things you can do which I can't do now, so you're going to have to help me get strong."

She said, "I will, Mom."

A Not So Random Act of Kindness

"So, how are you?"
"Hanging in there."
My tape recorder could have
shared the message.
It was always the same.

"Your legs are hairy.
Aren't you going home
this weekend for a visit?"
"Yes."
"Then you have to look your best."

Later, when she got off work,
Brenda showed up with a razor,
a can of shaving cream,
a basin of water.

Her hands lathered my legs,
turning to white
my thin limbs

withered from non-use,
tingling with nerve damage.

Gently, slowly,
taking care not to nick the skin,
she took broad strokes with the razor
and I watched row by row,
like a farmer plowing his fields,
one leg turned back to skin color.

"Your turn," she said,
and panic filled me.
Would I be able to reach
and hold the razor without
cutting myself? I looked to Brenda,
and her eyes gave me all the
encouragement I needed.

Love overflowed
in this simple act.

Smooth legs yes,
but the real results were unseen.
Caring for my needs,
she gave me dignity.

"Real Mom"

Monday, April 16th, Day 76

The moment of resurrection was not lost on me as I spent part of Easter afternoon at home. I was living the Pascal mystery—the life, death, and resurrection of Jesus. I left the tomb and stepped into the light to enjoy the freedom of home.

Becca met me at the door, and the smile on her face brought tears to mine. Hannah ran out of her room, repeating "Mama, Mama"—such music to my ears. I hugged her, savoring her little body in my arms again. Becca sat next to me on the couch for 10 minutes to watch *Little Rascals*. She told her pre-school class I was coming home to watch "Little Rascals," just like a real mom. Then, the girls had an Easter egg hunt.

Mary Beth, Tony's sister, gave me a quilt she had pieced together from squares made by all the family. Feeling wonderful and loved, I started crying. Becca could not understand my tears. Mary Beth said, "Becca, have you ever been so happy that you cried?"

She responded with a look of confusion and a shake of her head no. Smiles lit up the room, and it was good to be a part of family again.

Everyone got in the car and brought me back "home" to the hospital. How scary that I call this home! Part of me was sad to return, yet I knew I had to come back to this place, because I was exhausted and needed rest.

In the car, Becca kept asking, "Mom, when are you going to come home for good?" I answered that I would be home when I was healthy enough to come home. I told her it was okay to be sad and she could cry if she felt like it. I don't want her to keep her feelings inside.

Therapeutic Play

On Thursday nights, Mary Beth, Jeff, and their dog Kelsey would spend time with Becca, Hannah, and Sarah while Tony led music practice.

Jeff reenacted the grand adventures of John Smith from the Disney movie *Pocahontas* almost every week while the girls watched with great attention, giggling, and falling over each other on the couch. Then they would play the popcorn game, acting like puppies and catching popcorn in their mouths just like Kelsey. Because of the care of many people, the girls had a constant stream of love flowing to them, providing a sense of normalcy.

Yet, there was something amiss. After weeks of my absence, the girls' play took another form. The toy medical cart became the game of choice, Becca playing doctor and Hannah playing me. Then, they would switch roles, Hannah playing the doctor that made me well. Mary Beth and Jeff encouraged the girls to share their feelings and talk about me as much as they could. This therapeutic play helped the girls deal with the stress of my illness. Becca's preschool teacher also noticed that Becca played with the nurse's kit at school. Becca and Hannah learned through their play that doctors and nurses were helping me get well so I could come home.

Even still, Becca was often withdrawn when she came to visit. She would say hi and then find an activity to occupy herself. She would cry when she had to leave. When Becca passed a psychological evaluation with flying colors, the psych nurse felt her resiliency would help her bounce back into the happy little girl she had always been.

For the most part, the happy little girl came back with smiling eyes, a great sense of humor, and a big heart. Becca seemed to have weathered the storm of my illness well. But at age sixteen, a pattern emerged in Becca's behavior. We remembered that for the previous four years, Becca had been sick on Sarah's birthday. I believed this might have something to do with my illness, so I asked Becca, and she too thought there was a connection. We did some healing work together, learning that her inner child felt abandoned by me all those years ago. Becca remembered visiting the hospital and running through the cones, as well as riding up and down on my bed, but did not remember any other part of my hospital stay. When I came home, Becca experienced me differently than she did before Sarah's birth. I wasn't available for her in the same way. The little girl inside was stuck in the fear of losing her mother. Through guided meditation, Becca connected to her five-year-old self and reassured her that I was sorry—I never meant to leave her alone. She asked the little girl if it would be okay for me to hold her. I gathered Becca and her little self into my arms, and we cried together. Tears and the passing of time brought healing to us all.

In my own journey toward wholeness, I learned about kinesiology and using muscle testing as a way to tap into body wisdom. Sharing this knowledge with my daughters has been one of the greatest gifts to come out of my illness. With the practice of awareness, Becca is able to tap into her own innate wisdom and trust her feelings, knowing when she feels good about a decision and when to choose something different.

Last year, Becca experienced world travel as she studied abroad in Greece and Italy for a semester. I am proud of my daughter's strength, her ability to overcome obstacles, and her willingness to branch out on her own to discover the woman inside. My favorite picture from her trip is one of Becca standing on the coast of Greece, facing the ocean. Her arms are lifted up in gratitude, welcoming in all that life has to offer.

Mom's Journal,
Tuesday, April 18th Day 78

Jan moved into the transitional unit today. It is her final stop before going home. Dr. M is concerned about the amount of Percocet she is still taking for her knee and doesn't want her to become addicted to the medication. There has been no decision on knee surgery. Because her first PICC line clogged, the IV specialists worked for two hours in the middle of the night to put one in the other arm. Jan didn't sleep much. The t-shirts I fixed for Jan to wear are now for the wrong arm.

Mom's Journal,
Wednesday, April 19th   Day 79

Jan had another rough day. Her ileostomy pouch leaked, and the nurses are baffled about how to fix it. A feeding tube was sewn into the hole today, attached to the mesh covering Jan's wound. The nurses began feeding treatments through the tube.

Jan and Tony had a phone interview with Social Security—they need to know so much. Tony had to sign 14 sheets of paper to get Jan into the rehabilitation floor, because it is a Medicaid facility—a nursing home. No wonder Jan is so against being there—a nursing home!

Hannah visited today—seems to be much more at ease with Jan since she spent time at home. She sat on the bed and ate Jan's jell-O.

Wednesday, April 19th, Day 79

Mom told me tonight that I need to start thinking positively, and she's right. I have been down in the dumps for a couple of days. When I am mired in the muck, my thoughts get very confused. I know I should be positive, but bags and fluids and a bum knee are challenging day after day. I am in the midst of my own pity party; it is time to get out of this little slump, move on, and do what I need to do to get well.

Something Wrapped

WHEN I THINK OF SOMETHING WRAPPED, I THINK OF Christmas wrappings littering the floor among little bodies wrapped in robes playing with new toys and reading new books. Sparkly green paper with Santa or blue foil with snowflakes, these papers kept secrets away from little eyes until the right moment when, with joyous abandon, the wrappings were ripped off to find surprises underneath.

Now, I am taken back to another time when the

present was actually on the outside of the wrapping. I am the gift who is wrapped up in plastic wrap, sheets of pliable plastic covering my PICC line and protecting my wound. I am sitting in the strangest wheelchair I have ever seen. It is a molded mesh chair that makes a tic-tac-toe board on my back side. But I don't care. I bear the discomfort and hot stickiness of the plastic, because I know what is coming.

I am wheeled into a small hospital room with tile walls and a shower head. The nurse pulls my back toward the spout, turns the knob and adjusts the temperature, and then gently pushes me under the glorious spray of water.

Like little girls reveling in the newness of Santa gifts, I too am in heaven. I literally soak in the gift of water, the first time I have been under the delightful drops for more than ten weeks. The warmth cleanses me, washing away months of hospital beds, cold x-ray tables, sticky tape residue, and bodily fluids stuck on raw and tender skin. I close my eyes and my tears are lost in the wetness on my face.

I cry in joy, and I cry in pain, releasing pent-up emotions that find a safe place behind the sound of water in a tiny hospital bathroom. I rejoice in freedom from machines and relish the opportunity to be alone with my thoughts, away from constant beeps, away from the vigilant watch of nurses. I watch the drops roll away from my plastic clothing, gathering into the river of water traversing my body. I am flowing limitless to the beach and falling into rhythm with the waves. Breathing in and out, I feel tension slowly swirl down the drain.

Twenty minutes of bliss, and my skin is a prune. Withered limbs, already wrinkly from non-use, are more shriveled, like aging skin hanging on bone. The nurse takes me back to my room and rubs lotion into my arms and legs, smoothing the furrowed skin and allowing me to feel loved and deeply cared for. I close my eyes and unwrap the experience of water flowing like a river through my thoughts. The current lulls me to sleep.

Looking for Small Successes

Thursday, April 20th, Day 80

Kelly, the psych nurse, talked to me about searching for the good that will come out of this illness. She asked me to think about what I look forward to with hope in the next year. Nothing is going to be easy. I have to learn to be patient and look for the small accomplishments. It is easier said than done.

Sarah and Tony came up tonight. I held Sarah for a little while, but my arms tire easily, and I am sad I can't do more. Strength will return, but it is taking its sweet time.

Saturday, April 22nd, Day 82

I am growing new fingernails, and the new growth is pushing my old fingernails off the bed at the base of the nail. Every day, if there is time, my nurse will come in and painstakingly cut tape to fit my fingers and try to paste down the back of my nail. I am afraid of pulling a whole nail off before it is ready to fall off on its own.

Tony will become my primary caregiver when I go home. The house will be retrofitted with bars in the bathtub. Our futon bed is so low—I wonder how I will stand from a sitting position. I do not want to be handicapped, even though right now, I am "physically challenged." It's a nicer phrase.

Today, I saw progress. I stood all by myself without holding on to anything. No walker! What a confidence booster.

My sister-in-law, Mary Beth, told me about Hannah. The other night, when she and Jeff put Hannah in bed, she was upset and cried, "Do not leave me!"

Mary Beth lay down with her and said, "Do not worry honey, we are not going to leave you. We are going to be right outside."

Then, Sarah started sucking on her thumb and Hannah said, "What's that?"

Mary Beth said, "That is how Sarah comforts herself and makes herself feel better. Hannah, what makes you feel better?"

She said, "Mommy."

Mary Beth agreed. "You do have a nice mommy."

Hannah replied, "Um hmm."

Sunday, April 23rd, Day 83

Becca broke out in chicken pox, and now Tony will spend the week with her at home. This week, I'm working on a positive mindset. I want to be as self-sufficient as possible when I get out of here in two-and-a-half weeks.

Friday, April 28th, Day 88

With the strength I am gaining, I walked all the way to the end of the hall on crutches and didn't use the walker once.

I graduated back to full liquids today. This means I can have puddings and creamy soups. The wound is leaking less. My positive thinking helps.

The midwives came to see me today. They're planning a party for me on my last day here for all the doctors, nurses, and support staff that helped me to heal.

Sunday, April 30th, Day 90

It is time to get on with living. No more wishing my leg was better. The physical therapist is teaching me to walk with a bum leg. She made me walk 15 steps using only one crutch.

If Only...

If onlys
Float like silver clouds
on a stormy sky,
making promises of light
with no guarantees.

Empty words.

Everything will be fine.

If only I could walk without crutches on a leg
that bends.
If only my abdomen didn't leak.

If only I didn't have so many dressing changes a
day.

If only . . .

Would I sell my soul to the devil to make my
problems disappear?
What then?

The grass would be greener.

If only I could finish my book.
If only I had more money.
If only I didn't get angry with the girls.

If onlys
create more stress
in the present
by falsifying
the view of the future.

If onlys
keep me searching for
the destination
rather than
living the journey.

If only
I could live fully the moment
and appreciate the light around me.

Mom's Journal,
Wednesday, May 3, Day 93

Jan thinks the drainage around the catheter is slowing down—a good sign. Monday it was 1400 cc and Tuesday 700 cc. HALF! I hope someone didn't measure it wrong. She did talk to Dr. M about her knee. He said they won't do any surgery until her wound closes. Her physical therapist worked her hard today and got a bend of 49 degrees—a 9 degree improvement.

Thursday, May 4th, Day 94

We had a family conference with home health care specialists. I will have a nurse up to three times a day and occupational and physical therapy five times a week. There is also a nutritionist to teach me about the ileostomy and what kind of foods to eat.

For dinner last night, I ate a baked potato, a real treat! Today, I gobbled down mashed potatoes and tonight a banana. My PICC line was pulled, and I no longer have IVs in my arms. Goodbye TPN, my lovely intravenous nutrition! The feeding tube is all I have left. I've gone from eighteen tubes down to one. I feel free for the first time in months. What a journey I have been on!

I have a copy of the invitation to my party. It says, "Janet Haas is going home! Come help us celebrate!" I'm very excited. May 10th is circled in red on my calendar! Yes!

Mom's Journal,
Sunday, May 7th, Day 97

Jan and I talked this morning about how she got sick—didn't get very far until we were both in tears. She can only take a little a day, but it does give her a perspective on where she's been. She wonders why she was allowed to live.

Jan was home for a visit. She walked from the van into the family room with crutches—no wheelchair. Hannah and Sarah are broken out with chicken pox—they must be miserable. Two more days until she is home for good!

Home Sweet Home

Mom's Journal,
Wednesday, May 10th, Day 100!

The big day—Keith and I left Fort Collins at 6:00 a.m. in order to be at the hospital in time for all the festivities. We both commented on how different this trip was from the one we made to Denver 100 days ago.

Jan was dressed and ready when we got there but had to wait for the nurses to clamp off the feeding tube.

People from all over the hospital came to wish Jan well—the man from x-ray who transported Jan countless times, lab technicians who worked overtime to identify the cause of infection, doctors and nurses, respiratory therapists, physical and occupational therapists—I don't know if there was a person on staff who didn't know about Jan.

Everyone commented on the beautiful sunny day Jan had picked, especially considering the rainy weather we've had lately. We had a guest book where the staff wrote messages.

"When I first saw Jan, she looked like a bloated toad and today she looks like a princess!"

"Jan was so inspiring to take care of."

"You are a story not forgotten. Good luck".

"Cookie, you are one in a million! Love, Doughnut! "

"Good luck Jan. We're glad we can celebrate life with you."

"You are a great part of the team! You have done well. Someone upstairs loves you!"

"You will always be the most special patient I've ever had. There will always be a special place in my heart for you. I know you still have a lot to go through, but I know you can do it."

Mom's Journal,
Thursday, May 11th, Day 101

Jan was totally wiped out from her last hospital day on Wednesday. She sat in her chair all morning and enjoyed Hannah and Sarah who were still home with the chicken pox.

Jan napped on her futon with pillows all around her and did just fine. A visiting nurse came in the afternoon and changed her wound bag. Tony's job on the ileostomy bag is holding.

Between taking care of Sarah and Hannah and getting used to Jan's needs, Carol and I were exhausted by day's end. Mary Beth and Jeff came over—brought dinner and played with the girls.

Thursday, May 11th, Day 101

I am home! My first experience of sharing a family meal involves falling on my bum. Tony was helping me to the table by moving me up the one step into our kitchen eating area. Unfortunately, neither of us thought about the IV pole to which I was attached. IV tubing is strong, strong enough that when drawn taut, it pulled me back down off the step and flat onto my back side! Tears, both Tony's and mine, reminded us that we are learning how to manage my care in a completely new way.

The Right Combination of Skill and Prayer
Susan Callahan Grubaugh, family friend

At the time Jan was ill, I was expecting my own daughter, born a few months after Sarah. I knew who Jan was, and would see her in church with her daughters, two darling little pixies. Jan was one of those women who looked elegant and graceful even when nine months pregnant. Tony was a visible person in the parish so everyone knew when Jan had her baby girl. When we heard several days later that she had gone back into the hospital and was critically ill, we prayed, along with the rest of the MPB community, for her recovery. I thought often of the three little girls who needed their mother.

I had a good friend who was chief medical resident at the hospital through that winter and spring. I asked if she knew of Jan, and she said, "Oh, yes! Everyone in the hospital knows about Jan. She is the most critically ill patient here right now. She had no blood pressure when she came in; her heart stopped in the operating room, and she had to be resuscitated. When the surgeons opened her up, her abdomen was like one giant pus pocket."

Later in the year, my friend asked me about Jan, who was then home from the hospital. We spoke of our amazement at what Jan had survived. My doctor friend said, "As sick as she was, she really should have died."

I said, "She had an entire church and school praying for her. I really think that made the difference. I think it was a miracle."

My friend, an agnostic who was logical and self-determined, was uncomfortable with my statement and hastily backtracked a bit, "Oh, but she was young and healthy, and she had the very best medical care. Our hospital has the best emergency room and critical care staff in the city."

I agree that Jan had truly gifted and dedicated doctors and nurses. And I also know that the community at MPB tethered her to this world with our prayers while the doctors did their work.

Mom's Journal,

Saturday, May 13th, Day 103

It was a busy day. Carol took Becca shopping, and Hannah and Sarah went to Meg's house. It is truly a village that keeps this family afloat! Jan is very tired and depressed tonight—says the transitions are hard. She wants to get up and walk around without crutches and do things with the kids. She has been interacting with the girls a lot—feeding Sarah and singing to her and reading to Becca and Hannah. She enjoys being at home but it also makes her realize how much she can't do with them.

The drainage seems to be less, and we are trying to get Jan to eat more. Nothing really sounds good, so we have to force eating. Tony is helping Jan with her physical therapy exercises on the floor now. She has to do her work twice a day. She is exhausted after each session.

Mom's Journal
Sunday, May 14th, Day 104
Mother's Day! Jan told me yesterday that if she could, she would buy me the biggest Mother's Day gift ever for all I've done for her. I told her she has already given me the greatest gift, her life. More tears. We have been shedding tears regularly!

We had a nice meal to celebrate the day. Jan ate mashed potatoes, turkey, fruit, and a little broccoli. She gets very tired, even from eating. She has been so focused on the work of coming home, and now she is experiencing some normal family activities. It takes a lot of her energy.

She is walking more to the bathroom and bedroom than she did in the hospital. When she fell two days ago, I was very concerned it would slow her down. Her seat is sore, but she is not letting it stop her much.

Tuesday, May 16th, Day 106
It is a good thing Mom is here to help me adjust to being home. Even though a nurse comes twice a day, the extra care I need falls on her. Today, she helped me shower, shave my legs,

change the ileostomy bag, and over two-and-a-half hours passed. We both needed naps. Aunt Doris came to take Mom to the store and left me for 30 minutes—I did fine. I took two walks today, gaining a little confidence in my movement.

When we changed the wound bag today, we measured the wound. It is now seven-and-a-half inches long and one-and-a-half inches wide. This is a huge improvement from when I first saw it in the hospital. The drainage seems to be going down.

Wednesday, May 17th, Day 107

I love being home! The sound of laughter and play, little girl hugs, and just being in their presence helps heal me. If only I could concentrate on the joy of little girls and not be bothered with medical baggage!

The worst part of being here is the constant reminder of things I can't do—dance with the girls, lie on the floor and tickle them, eat regular food in regular portions. I can feel the weight of my recovery, like a lead apron upon my chest. I don't want to do the hard work of healing, yet I know the only way out of this IS to do the work. I want my life to be easy. Unfortunately, I know that deep down, giving up and giving in is not the answer.

The Hairband

Almost late for school again
so I take the brush,
move it through Becca's hair,
and for a moment, I am caught up
in the smell and softness of the

brown mane in front of me.

Tony sighs heavily.
The clock is ticking away
and so is his patience.

I brush Becca's hair into a ponytail,
holding it with one hand
while stretching the hair band
as far as my fingers will go.

The moment takes me back to the hospital
to the very first time
it took five minutes of concentration
to touch each of my fingers,
one at a time
to my thumb.

Now I want my fingers to work together
stretching the band.
Yet it is not big enough to pull hair through.
I fall short of the task
and Becca's hair falls back around her face.

My spirits fall with my tears,
reminding me
of this healing journey.
My fingers are just one indication
of how far I have yet to go,
how much work it will take
to find normal.

Friday, May 19th, Day 109

My ileostomy seal just broke again this morning. Bags! Bags! Bags! I am a bag lady! I'm so TIRED of all these fluids and bags!

Saturday, May 20, Day 110

Bonnie Brae Ice Cream! My first venture out other than to a doctor! The cinnamon ice cream in my kiddy cone tasted like heaven and reminded me of Tony's and my first date. How lucky I am to have such a wonderful man in my life! I wouldn't be here without his love and concern. Another man might have left me during this crisis. But Tony took his wedding vows, "In sickness and in health," seriously. I thank God for his patience, kindness, and ability to see the good in all things.

Sunday, May 21, Day 111

Writing thank you notes to those who have sent words of encouragement is a nice way to pass the time. I just wrote to my friend Sue who was the choir director at St. Pius X Church in Cedar Rapids, Iowa, the first church Tony worked as a liturgist. I can count on a card from Sue almost every week. The notes are full of love and God's presence, and they arrive just when my spirits need a lift. Some cards from friends make me laugh and others make me cry. It is good to feel connected to a wider community.

As Tony was helping me with my ileostomy bag, we were wondering how much longer we will have to deal with the illness. A whole year of my life to recuperate from an infection seems insurmountable.

I've heard the saying, "God doesn't give you more than the

two of you can handle." I'd like to give God a piece of my mind about what I can and can't handle. I'd like to know where God is hanging out when we are mopping up the drainage from my belly with rolls and rolls of gauze. It wouldn't be a pretty conversation.

OK, I guess that's not fair, because I really never even liked that saying. It's as if God is up in heaven doling out punishments and challenges, because there is nothing better to do. I don't believe that for a second. I just find it hard to recognize God's presence sometimes. Bad things just happen, and I am learning through this experience. I'm not always the most eager learner, that's for sure, and I get frustrated *every single day!* That's part of being human. Somehow, I need to look beyond the suffering to the good that is coming out of this experience. Deep down, I know that while this is difficult, I am never alone.

> For Jesus, healing was a manifestation of God's great love and compassion for all of us. Had Jesus believed that illness and suffering were sent from God for our good, he would never have intervened in God's process. Thus, it is obvious that he did not subscribe to this belief—even if we are tempted to do so at times.
> - Linda Smith,
> *Called into Healing*

TEARS COME FRESH TO MY EYES AS I REREAD CARDS WRITTEN over 16 years ago. So many cards put away in a box, filled with love and prayers for my successful healing. Cards from people I didn't even know who somehow found out about me through a friend or family member. From a hospital bed, the story of my fight to live made its way across the country and into the hearts of many people. What is it that made so many people stop and write? "You don't know me but you are in my prayers." "I heard about you from _____ and wanted to let you know that I put you on the prayer chain in our church."

I remember once when a cousin was visiting me in the hospital. We talked about the power of prayer and the power of six degrees of separation. He was convinced that most of Denver was praying for me across the network of churches and businesses where someone knew someone who knew someone. What about my story was worthy of such attention? Was it that I was a young mom fighting to live, so I could spend my life with my three little girls? I believe that many people could put themselves in our shoes, as either the mom with babies or the husband taking care of a sick spouse. But I believe there was a power beyond understanding that made my story spread and ignite the hearts of people who heard it. It was the power of prayer, the unseen energy of thoughts lifted up to the only One who could take all those prayers, multiply them, and spread them like a safety net under us, so as we swung on the trapeze between life and death, there was never a doubt that life would win out.

The children at the parish school prayed daily for me, Becca's mom, and they took their prayers and concerns home to their own families, where people lit candles and kept vigil with Tony. The day I went home, the principal talked to the whole school about how their prayers helped me, and even though our three little girls had chicken pox, they were excited to have their mom home. I have often thought about how the principal would have handled telling 500 children that I had died. Obviously, that wasn't meant to happen. Crayons and messages from students color many of the notes in my keepsake box.

Even now, rereading the cards, I feel the power of prayer once again lay down the safety net below me, reminding me that I am never alone, and even when I stumble, there is a whole community of people who love and care for me and my family. Why do I deserve this? None of us deserves God's grace, yet maybe in the way I have lived my life, trusting that God would somehow provide for our needs, I am able to see the network of people that have always been around me.

Tony and I built a network with kind words and actions, over and over again, so that when we ourselves were in need, people rose to the occasion and helped. I like the image of so many people picking up their shovels and doing their part to move the mountain that was in front of me. This was never a solo effort, and this book was never meant to be just about my survival. It has always been for the wider community, so that they may understand the power of prayer, the power of stepping up and doing what needs to be done, and the power of love to conquer darkness.

There is nothing better than a kind note from a friend or a stranger to bring a smile to one's face. The words of so many cards seep into my soul and remind me that God's love works mysteriously, not only in the present time, but also across time and space to bring healing to a young mother fighting for her life, or a stranger in need of a sign that they are never alone.

Monday, May 24th, Day 114

Right now, I'm filling out more paper work for Social Security, and it is degrading. "How much do you listen to the radio or watch TV? What type of programs do you listen to or watch? Are you able to remember and understand these programs?" I know this is the information they need. I have to go back 10 years to do my work history and tell them different things like, "How much weight was lifted? How much walking did I do? How much standing? How much sitting? How much bending? " I will fill out the forms to help my family survive with me not working. Long-term disability would be a blessing.

Yesterday, the physical therapist measured a 51-degree bend in my knee, and my hip flexion was up to 115.

I went to see Dr. P this afternoon. I can graduate from using the feeding tube for 24 hours a day to just 12. He was impressed by the healing of the wound and my food intake. I feel happy with a good report. For the first time since I got home from the hospital, I am sitting in my chair and there is no IV pole standing next to me. The girls don't have to fight their way around a pole to get to me for goodnight hugs and kisses. I'm feeding four-month-old Sarah her bottle right now. She is getting very sleepy. But she is staring at me and smiling. I feel a surge in our mother-daughter bond.

If I remember correctly, it took me two weeks on the rehabilitation floor before I felt like I was making progress. Then something clicked, my mood changed and life was better. That's where I am now. I am working through this transition.

In the Midst of Community

Sunday, May 28th, Day 118

Today was my first trip back to Most Precious Blood Church since I've been sick. I loved being part of the community again. At the end of the service, Fr. Ken said, "Now, I know she probably doesn't want me to do this, but we've been praying for this person for a long time, and I just want you all to know she is here today."

He introduced me and said, "We just have to thank you. I'm so glad you're here. We thank you because you have changed us as a community." When they clapped, I cried.

Deacon Lou came up and said, "It is an honor to give you communion. I am so happy for you and glad you're back." He had big tears in his eyes. He almost forgot to say, "The Body of Christ." He said "God Bless You" and was handing me the host, and then he remembered and said, "Oh, oh, the Body of Christ." Deacon Lou was in his 80s, still full of life, and a great role model of service to the community.

When my bandages started leaking during mass, I was very concerned about what would happen when I stood up. By the time we finished saying good-bye at church, and I walked all the way out to the car, my dressings were hanging in my panties. The emotions of the day caught up to me, and I cried again.

How easily tears of joy and gladness mix with the tears of frustration at a leaking wound.

A Community Gathers
Rita Mailander, currently Director of Religious Education at MPB

Communities can be places of great comfort and support. I like to think of our parish community as a well, offering refreshment and vital replenishment to thirsty souls. That can come in many forms. In the case of Jan's illness, the community rallied around the young family with prayers, food, childcare, and other daily necessities. Early in Jan's illness, the parish held an evening of prayer to lift up the whole family for divine grace. Other young mothers who were friends of Jan organized the evening.

One of the pleas was not only for prayers offered on behalf of the Haas family, but also blood donated in Jan's name. One of our parishioners who suffered from mental illness attended the evening. I am sure she felt this was her way to pay back some of the many prayers that had been offered on her behalf and it was a way of belonging and contributing to something bigger than herself. As the prayer aspect of the evening was drawing to a close and the announcement for the blood drive was being made, this good soul stood and announced to the congregation how essential it was that we donate blood specifically designated for Jan Haas. She said that blood banks often substituted monkey blood for human blood if there was a shortage of donors. This declaration left the presiders of the evening speechless and perplexed. It's hard to transition a proclamation such as that! They merely emphasized the desire for a successful blood drive and concluded the evening.

My 10-year-old daughter attended the prayer service with me and on the way home expressed her confusion about monkey blood transfusions. I tried to explain that though the woman's information of blood bank operations was false and fear-based, her intentions were good.

After all, that woman came out on a cold winter's night to pray for a young woman that she did not know personally and to offer whatever insight into life that she possessed. She came to be part of a community that generated goodness and strength. She must have known that she needed to drink from the well too and tried, however feebly, to replenish it.

Communities are made up of those who have been recipients of grace from each other. My mom used to have a saying: "Not being ignorant of sorrow, I can appreciate the sorrows of others." Though the story of the monkey blood precaution holds humor, it also holds tenderness. One who was wounded reached out to another wounded one and offered whatever wisdom she had available. Surely a good and merciful God hears the sincerity of heart and grants healing to both.

Wednesday, May 31st, Day 121

Kelly has been visiting every week, following my progress. She said the people at the hospital still ask about me. The SICU nurses passed along their love. Dr. P was in ICU the other day bragging about how good my wound looks. Kelly said, "You know, you are just one of those people that affects many others."

She was glad to hear the good news about the 70-degree bend in my knee. I told her I didn't know why it was getting better. Maybe it is the magnesium I'm taking. She said, "There's a cartoon about two men going across a big gorge, making a wooden bridge. The bridge isn't finished, yet it's still crossing the gorge, even though they are only working from one end. They're looking at each other. One guy is carrying a load of wood, and the other guy is hammering nails. The man carrying the wood says, "Don't think about why it's working. Just keep hammering!"

Thursday, June 1st, Day 122

A field trip at the park was the plan for Becca's last day of preschool. Tony and I loaded up the van and went to watch them play. Walking across the park and having the sun warm my body felt so good. One of the mothers, a nurse, said, "Welcome to the real world! The hospital is not the real world."

The sky is so blue on this beautiful day! I'm so glad to be here, so glad God has given me a second chance at life. May I never take for granted all the things that I CAN do!

Tuesday, June 6th, Day 127

My friend Kathy has been here since Saturday. It has been great to renew our friendship. Kathy and I met my first year teaching at All Souls Catholic School in Cedar Rapids, Iowa. I was replacing a well-loved teacher who was moving out of state in the middle of the year. Kathy taught the other 5th grade class.

Daily, I heard, "That's not the way Mrs. ___ did it!" Kathy helped me stay true to myself and teach the kids with my own style and classroom management. We became instant friends. I can still see her sitting across from us when Tony and I asked her to be Becca's godmother. Her face lit up, and she practically jumped out of her chair. When she heard about my illness, she planned a visit.

She is at the park with the girls right now. She's been washing and folding clothes, fixing dinner, and finding things to do without being asked. I am touched by how many friends I have who are willing to pitch in and do the boring stuff.

The bad part is I haven't felt very good the last couple of days. A sinus infection is zapping my energy. Getting up from the bed and going to the bathroom or walking out to the family room makes me sweaty and lightheaded.

The Ileostomy

Just inches above my hip bone
two red lips oddly stick out of me.
Because of IT,
I maintain a normal function of the body:
waste elimination.
Do I befriend it?
Or am I angry IT exists?

Eat Jan, or you know what will happen!
Three pounds less and my hip bone rises.
Pop! Another leaking bag.

Midnight.
Tony sleepily cuts a new opening.
Not too big or the skin will burn away,
but not too small, get all of IT in.
We paste over swollen flesh,
trying to seal
hills and valleys of skin and bones.

I pray for daylight.

Two a.m.
A warm rush of excrement floods over my skin.
I scream at the burning,
half in anger and half in pain.
We start with a new seal again.

Curse you, hip bone!
Curse you, excrement!
Curse the war of my body
and the sleepless dark nights where
battles are seldom won.

God help me! Make this night end!
Give me peace…peace…peace.

Mother God's arms surround me.
When the sun rises,
even the battleground looks peaceful.

Cries in the Night

I LAY DOWN IN BED, PILLOWS UNDER MY LEGS AND ELBOWS. Sleeping on my back with my legs raised kept my abdomen as stable as possible. The ileostomy and the wound on my belly prevented me from side sleeping. There was barely room for Tony on the futon we shared.

Exhausted by a busy day, I held Tony's hand, grateful that he and I were walking this journey together. His calming presence slowed my breathing, my shoulders relaxed into the pillows. With Tony's hand in mine and his strength supporting me, I fell into a light sleep.

Shortly past midnight, I felt the familiar warm sting of liquid waste flow down my side. The seal under my ileostomy bag had sprung a leak. We began the 15-minute ritual to repair the seal.

When my weight was stable, the stoma, where waste exited my body, rested on a slight hill, and the skin barrier under the waste collection bag created a tight seal. However, my weight would often decrease 10 pounds or more in a matter of days, and my hip bone would pop up, creating a valley below the skin barrier. Leaking and painful burning would ensue. What followed was the removal of the sticky skin barrier from very red, raw skin, cutting a hole in the new barrier just the right size of the stoma, and placing it over skin crying to be left alone. A new collection bag was then attached, much like one seals a lid on a plastic bowl. A normal ileostomy only needs to be changed every four days, yet my fluctuating weight and the slightest movement in bed created a multitude of opportunities to practice cutting just the right size hole in the skin barrier.

With the ileostomy barrier changed, and a new absorbent pad placed beneath me, Tony and I closed our eyes, hoping for rest, but this night had a few more surprises for us.

Yet again, I felt the familiar rush of caustic liquid on my raw skin, waking me from a fitful sleep. It would be a night where the skin was too raw, the seals would not hold, and our patience wore very thin.

Two more times Tony and I practiced our doctoring skills in the middle of the night. Our bodies were exhausted to the point that no amount of sleep would make the weariness fade away. The warm excrement was no match for the hot tears that flowed down my face, and the burning on my skin couldn't compete with the scorching fire of anger and frustration boiling inside of me.

Shortly after we changed the seal and bag for the fourth time, baby Sarah cried out from the girls' bedroom. Five months old, it was odd for her to wake up at night, but she too was restless, maybe sensing our agitation. She whimpered and settled back to sleep. Five minutes later, she let out a piercing cry and wouldn't stop.

Tony pulled back the covers, and in his frustration cried out, "I am going to kill her!"

"No," I screamed, grabbing his arm, "Don't hurt

her!"

Assuring me he had come to his senses and was not about to hurt Sarah, I let him go to care for her needs. Tears of anxiety and relief fell onto my pillow.

This event would later bring rolls of laughter and stress reduction to our family. Yet, now, I was caught in the middle of the frustration. The enormity of my health situation moved me to constantly worry about the future, something I couldn't control. The excrement running down my side forced me back into the present to take care of the task at hand. Tony had already lived months of my hospitalization in survival mode, one day and one moment at a time.

I couldn't change what was happening to me, but I could adjust my focus. When I finally settled down to sleep, I found peace lying in God's arms.

A Three-Day Stay

Friday, June 9th, Day 130

The sun is streaming through my window, waking me up to a new day. But I am not in my bed at home next to Tony. I am waking up in the hospital yet again. The hot summer weather, allergies, a sinus infection, and the pulling of the feeding tube have contributed to severe dehydration. My electrolytes are out of balance, causing a reentry into the hospital, this time at a different hospital where my family doctor practices. I am away from all the other doctors and nurses that know and love me.

I had been losing energy all week. My lightheadedness and weakness forced me to be taken in a wheelchair into Dr. M's office. My almost non-existent blood pressure and rapid heartbeat made Dr. M think about septic shock, one of the conditions the doctors fought when I was first admitted to the hospital. I was paranoid about being sick. After a few tests, he admitted me.

In my spacey, tired state, I felt like I was facing a huge setback that would keep me in the hospital for months. I wanted no part of it. I told Tony I was losing my will to fight. I was ready to let go and ease into death.

The look was only there a brief moment—deep-seated anger flashed across Tony's face, as if to say, "You are sure as hell going to fight! You didn't get well enough to go home only to give up on me and the girls!"

I read the message loud and clear. Giving up on life was not one of my options.

I WAS ON THE FAMILY PRACTICE FLOOR UNTIL ABOUT 1:30 in the morning. The wound was too much for the nurses to handle—draining so quickly, dressings had to be changed every two hours. I was sent to the coronary care unit.

Five nurses quickly attended to me, taking my temperature, attaching me to the heart monitor and blood pressure machines. I am not sure why I was put here instead of the regular intensive care unit. Lucky for me, Dr. M was in the hospital delivering a baby and came to see me. It took quite a bit of convincing on Dr. M's part to assure the nurses I wasn't in any cardiac danger. Reluctantly, they moved the noisy machines out of the room.

The nurse wanted to call Tony and let him know I had been moved.

"Let him sleep," I said.

The shocked nurse looked at me and said, "I don't think you understand. Do you know where you are? You are in the surgical intensive care unit, actually the coronary care unit." She tried to emphasize how serious this was! "You are in intensive care."

I said, "Yes."

She said, "And you don't want to call your husband?"

I replied, "No, this is nothing compared to where I have been. Tony will find me in the morning. I've been in ICU before. I can handle this, and Tony needs his sleep."

I know it was a little gesture, letting Tony sleep. I had so little power to give Tony a break from our hectic lives, and this was one way I could pay back Tony for all the sleepless nights he had already spent in a hospital chair. My sleepless night couldn't compare to all the ones he had endured. Sleeping in a comfortable bed at home was the one gift I could give.

Getting In Nutrients

How will we feed you, the doctors ask?
The hole in your intestine is a problem.

Tell me something I don't know.

Insert a feeding tube
and stitch the rubber against the skin.
Maybe the wound will heal
around the foreign invader
sticking out of my abdomen.
It's a crap shoot.
They don't know what to do
anymore than I understand
why this happened to me.

Liquid nutrition! Yum!
What's your pleasure?
My imagination draws up
strawberry shortcake today,
maybe chocolate malt tomorrow.
Yet the white liquid
squeezed into a tube
cannot tickle my taste buds.

What about real food,
a feast for my senses?
I imagine sitting at table
partaking of food and wine—
a fine dining experience.

Fresh basil and garlic
dress the chicken,
lemon juice over
summer's colorful vegetables,
butter melting over a whole grain roll,
a symphony of flavors.

My mouth waters just thinking about
a small dark morsel of the
chocolate brownie
melting over my tongue.

Now I imagine my body
digesting as it should,
food traveling through a healthy system,
leaving the body normally.

Unfortunately,
broccoli bits
pouring out my belly
snap me back to reality.
Not really a feast for my senses—
instead a bad dream playing itself
over and over again.

Saturday, June 10th, Day 131

This will always be the year that changed us in ways we'll
never be able to completely understand. I ask God to give us the
wisdom, strength, and courage to make good out of this situation.
I can't believe I am suffering like this for nothing. I do realize how
close I came to losing everything, of not even being here to cry
and complain about my life. I'm in tears thinking about losing all
that I have now. I know how depressed I must have been when I
first came to the hospital again. I was scared and glad to find out
that I was just severely dehydrated. I don't ever want to give up.

The hospital chaplain came to see me while Tony was here,
and was quite interested in my story. He repeated over and over
again, "Oh my, Oh dear, Oh my, Oh dear, Oh dear. You've

been through it all, haven't you?" It was a blessing to feel God's presence as the chaplain held our hands and prayed with us. I haven't been able to pray for myself. I still feel numb when it comes to talking to God.

I know God is with me. I know that I'm not walking this alone, but I get so angry and I want to scream, "Why me, Why? Why? Why?" I can see the beautiful mountains out my window, and I wish I could climb the highest one and scream at the top of my lungs. I would echo my anger through the foothills, express my frustration about being sick, and wish to wake up from this nightmare.

Then, I would take a minute to breathe and thank God for giving me the opportunity to voice my truth. I'd thank God that I am still alive and that from somewhere deep within, I am finding the strength to take on the challenges of every new day.

Storming Heaven

The question "Why?" hung over my head
and for a thought-filled pause,
I had a desire to touch heaven,
to knock on the gates
and make my appointment with God.

I did not desire a lengthy stay,
only a precious moment,
face-to-face with God
to get some answers,
to know the reason for my suffering.

But alas, (un) lucky for me,
the prayers were so many
and the angels too thick
to let me through.

A community of family,
friends and strangers have been
storming heaven with prayers.

So the questions still exist.
One thing is clearer now.
Answers are not mine to know.

I walk on,
searching, reaching,
finding a hand to hold and guide me
through the mysterious darkness.
I am not alone.

Monday, June 12th, Day 133

I was only in the hospital for three days. In order to fight dehydration, Dr. M has me drinking an electrolyte solution all the time instead of water. I've tried several different kinds, and now I'm drinking Pedialyte with a little bit of lemon in it. It's tolerable. I can actually guzzle it like water. It beats the upset stomach I got from salted Gatorade.

Wednesday, June 14th, Day 135

There is an amazing network of people from church helping us on our journey. Today, someone I barely know scrubbed and cleaned my kitchen floor while keeping me company. It is a humbling experience to have people clean while all I do is sit. A friend commented the other day how strange it is to know which drawer holds Tony's underwear. People have become intimately involved in our lives. I look forward to the day I get to pay it forward to someone else who needs help.

Community Hands and Prayer
Fr. Ken Koehler, Pastor at MPB Parish during this time

Each day that the prayers continued, people in the community began to find ways to help Tony and assist in the care of Sarah, and eventually help Jan. I can hardly believe so many people gave a whole day to care for the girls and to prepare meals for the rest of the family. These were activities that took care of daily needs. It was not something that passed quickly but rather strengthened as time went on. More importantly, the gatherings of prayer not only helped Jan in recovery but truly became a support for Tony. Science has given some indication that prayer works. It gave strength to Jan to heal, and it gave support to Tony and Jan and their family to not lose hope.

As I sat in my chair in our family room and watched volunteers from the church fold laundry and clean my house, I wondered what I did to deserve this kind of love. I had forgotten that I didn't need to DO anything to be worthy.

As difficult as it was to allow others to help, I had no choice. There was no way I was capable of doing the tasks of running a house. And I knew that there would be no time in the near future when I could reciprocate their generosity. The only gift I could give was my willingness to set aside my ego and accept the help of many people. My allowing became my giving in this exchange for the friendship and helping hands of volunteers. I welcomed others to share their gifts and their love. This interaction speaks volumes about the importance of community.

Years later, when volunteering my time as a Healing Touch Practitioner, I worked with a woman who had cancer. I remember talking with her about the pain of her illness, something she chose to bear by herself. While she was reaching out to strangers to help her through the difficult time, she did not share all the details of her cancer with her community of friends and family. So many times, she talked about feeling completely alone. I remember days when I felt alone in doing the work of healing, but I was never alone in spirit. My suffering was made public, and because of that, my healing was public, too. As a result, I was not the only one who was healed.

> The I in illness is isolation, and the crucial letters in wellness are we.
>
> - Author unknown, as quoted by Mimi Guarneri, *The Heart Speaks: A Cardiologist Reveals the Secret Language of Healing*

Sunday, June 18th, Day 139

My friend Mary from Cedar Rapids left today after spending four days with me. You know someone is a true friend when you pick up where you left off and keep right on going! She helped our family immensely, giving my other caregivers a much-needed respite. She saw me at my worst and shared her love and compassion.

The other night, we were watching "Forest Gump," and Tony cried at the end. I could see tears coming down his face. Tony never cries. He tried to hide it. Even when I gave him a Kleenex, he ignored it, saying, "I don't need one." Later, I said, "Tony, you cried in the movie."

He responded, "Yes, I did."

I asked "Why?"

"Jan, it just hits too close to home. It's too real for me."

He couldn't handle it when Jennie died in the movie. I am used to seeing strong, stoic Tony. I know he was scared of losing me and he is living this nightmare, too, only in a different way. It's nice to know he can express his feelings and not keep everything inside. Mom said, "You know, if you don't weep on the outside, your body weeps on the inside." I hope he is sharing his experience with someone.

Tony has been the guiding light that has seen me through this ordeal. As much as I want him to express his feelings, I still need him to be strong now. I don't think I could handle his tears on a regular basis.

❧

I was hoping to be recovering from the short hospital stay by now, but my blood pressure has been very low for three days. At my doctor's appointment, the nurse couldn't even get my blood pressure when I was sitting up, which would explain why I am dizzy. According to the tests, I am still dehydrated.

Round Three

Wednesday, June 21st, Day 142

I'm at the hospital again for the third time. I came in yesterday and was held in observation for 23 hours until the doctors decided they didn't know what was wrong with me and admitted me to the hospital. My ileostomy output has been very watery and quite abundant. I'm not sure what the doctors are going to do, but I refuse to go home and come back in two weeks again dehydrated. I want to be well when I go home.

Taking Back Control

What is different
about this hospital stay
than my first 100 days?

I am different,
learning to take care of myself.

Severe dehydration
made veins difficult to locate
and an IV in my hand
was the only solution.

Inconvenient.
Painful.
Not a long-term solution.

So now that I am staying…

"I want you to change the IV site.
Pull it out and before you put it back in,
I am going to take a long hot shower."

The words roll off my tongue like an order
and the nurses look at me,
nervous about unhooking me from the IV,
nervous about me in a shower by myself,
wondering
"Who is this patient
who has the courage
to stand up for her own needs?"

It is me,
Jan,
learning how to be a person first
in a world where often
patients are just an illness to treat.

Friday, June 23rd, Day 144

Dr. W, or Sherlock as I like to call him, is on the scene again and has narrowed down my current hospitalization to three things. I've been put on a high-fat diet to see how well I absorb fat. His next possibility is that I have an overabundance of bacteria in the intestine, although the latest round of antibiotics should have helped. The third reason is infection, but he isn't sure why or where. I'm glad he is on the case. He is an excellent doctor with a fun-loving personality. He is my Sherlock Holmes, searching every clue and investigating every possibility. I know he will get to the bottom of this!

Kelly Gaul came to see me. She continues to bless me with her gift of time and wisdom. I told her that Tony and I want to go on a retreat at the end of this journey so we can get the grief out of our system. She said, "Jan, you know, this is never going to be 'out of your system.'" The illness you experienced and the trauma you are going through is like putting a new ring on your finger. You feel it all the time. It bothers you because you can't stop thinking about the ring on your finger and how it doesn't fit right. It just doesn't feel right. After a while, the ring fits. That feeling goes away, but the ring stays."

Maybe eventually, when I look back at this time, I won't have so many emotions wrapped up in the experience. The grief will eventually disappear, but the memory of this time will always be with me. As Tony says, our job is to embrace it, integrate it, and allow this experience to make us more whole. I don't know about the embracing part, but eventually, I hope to find my way to wholeness.

❧

The city lights were nice tonight. Tony and I played backgammon for a while and just enjoyed each other's company. I have a good view of the city and the mountains.

> My eyes wander from my hospital bed
> on the ninth floor
> to the window where
> a setting sun hides behind gray clouds,
> peeking through cracks
> creating silver white linings and streaks of light
> across the sky.
> It is an answer to prayer.
> A Divine message:
> I am with you.

Three-Sided Containers

HOW FUNNY THAT A CLEAR, THREE-SIDED CONTAINER could bring about such laughter from the family.

One of my daily activities was to measure the liquid output of the ileostomy. I collected the drainage in a three-sided, clear container with measurements on the side. Of course, the girls wanted to know what I was doing and so we told them in language they understood. "The doctors want to know how much poop Mom has, so I have to measure it." To young children, that was pretty clear.

Now, back in the hospital, I was hoping for some answers for the high volume of output from the ileostomy. In the meantime, I was happy I was moving better. Several times a day, a nurse would push the IV pole beside me while I walked with my crutches, cruising around the nurse's station like laps around a track. While I was taking one of my daily spins, I noticed a nurse drinking a Coke out of a strangely familiar triangular container. It struck me as funny how a different hospital used the containers in a way that seemed strange in comparison to what I was used to.

One day not long after this experience, my mom decided to make two containers of sun tea. I had a nice sunny window where it would brew quickly in the familiar triangular-shaped containers. Iced tea would be a refreshing treat.

When Tony and the girls came in that afternoon for a visit, Tony said, "Give me one of those things. I'd like to drink some of that tea."

I handed the container to Tony as Becca looked on, crinkling her face in puzzlement.

I started laughing and said, "Becca, you know what Mom uses those containers for?"

"Yes," she said.

"Well, that's just iced tea," I assured her.

Hannah, who had been playing and not paying attention turned around and looked at Tony and said, "Dad, you're not going to drink Mom's poop, are you?"

The tears poured down my face from laughter, allowing me to build up some much needed healing endorphins!

Saturday, June 24th, Day 145

After eating standard American fare for two days—hamburgers, French fries, and chocolate shakes, I put out 6000 cc of waste in 24 hours. Sherlock believes my body is not absorbing fat like it should. I am glad to be going back to a simpler low-fat diet to see if that helps.

Sunday, June 25th, Day 146

The girls and Tony just left after visiting me for a while. I want to jump in the car and go home with them.

Becca keeps saying, "Mom, why can't you go home with us? When are you going to get better?"

I remember that as tough as it is to see the girls, and as tough as it is to be without them, they are the reason I am strong. They are the reason that I have to get better. Oh, when will it end?

SPENDING TIME AWAY FROM FAMILY WAS THE MOST difficult part of my healing. My favorite hobby was my family—I wanted to be a part of whatever activities they were involved in. I continued to question where this illness came from and why it kept me from home for so long. I know I didn't deserve to suffer, to redeem myself from some past event in my life. God didn't work that way. I wasn't conscious of asking for any kind of lesson—especially one to be taught through such a traumatic experience. I did know that on some level I would have to accept where I was in order to move forward.

Several people that year counseled me to consider a lawsuit against the hospital. Yet, no matter how often I relived Sarah's birth in my mind, I couldn't find a person to blame. I could only think of the doctors, nurses, and support staff who worked countless hours to bring me back to life. A lawsuit would have kept me focused on the illness rather than working to bring about healing. Money would not have healed my body. Only time and love would do that.

Monday, June 26th, Day 147

I've been waiting all morning for my CAT scan. The nurse came in this morning at 6:30 a.m. to have me drink my second glass of Gastrografin, which tasted like lemonade, so at least it wasn't barium.

The dietician just came in and talked to me again about my inability to absorb fat. She said the high output may mean I'm not able to absorb ANY fat at all. Even though I'm on a low-fat diet,

> Teach us to believe
> that by your grace
> all shall be well, and all
> shall be well,
> and all manner of
> things shall be well.
> Amen.
> - St. Julian of Norwich

I may have to cut down almost completely, and she suggested maybe possibly even going back to a feeding tube just to get the nutrients I need.

Sherlock hasn't made his decision yet about what I'll be doing. He is waiting to see what the CAT scan shows. I can stand anything for a while, even no fat, as long as I'm making progress toward getting healthy. I am dizzy from my walk. I think it could be because I'm hungry and I'm still losing so much fluid. Every day, my condition remains the same but we are searching for answers. I am learning to survive one day at a time.

Tuesday, June 27th, Day 148

The ileostomy bag came off four times in the middle of the night, and I had to be stuck with needles while the nurses tried to find a new IV site. It took them three or four tries, and each poke hurt so much. The antibiotics I am taking make my veins roll away from needles instead of staying still.

Mom called and prayed over the phone with me. I feel better.

Mother God

God came to me
as the love of a fierce mother

with wild eyes and dark skin,
a mother protecting her child.
This God was not to be crossed.

Mother God,
strong enough to hold back the tide
of the impending storm,
stopping the wind
with the wave of Her hand.

The supple softness of skin
and flesh enfold me—
I am cradled in
my Mother's arms.

Healing white light,
ribbons of pure love
wrap around me
again and again,
creating a cocoon,
a space for healing.

Mother God
came to me
in my greatest need.
I invited Her to stay.

The doctors talked about putting in a central line for IV fluids. I weigh 146 pounds again, and my feet are swollen. It has to be from fluid, so I don't know how I can be dehydrated.

◦❦◦

Because of my shortened bowel, I have a hormone secreting way too much stomach acid. Where normal people would have a hormone level of 200, I have a hormone level of 500. Sherlock gave me a magic purple pill to counteract the hormone. Another pill in the morning should give us results in the afternoon.

The fat absorption study still isn't done. As a matter of fact, the sample was mailed to Minnesota, and when Sherlock came in he announced, "Well, your stool is in Minnesota at the Mayo Clinic." It just sounded funny. I can't believe they sent the whole 6000 cc sample. He was still chuckling about that the next day. He said, "You know, I just don't feel right about you and your stool being in different states. I think I'll have them send it back if you'd like." He's such a joker!

Just when I think I am walking this journey alone, someone like Sherlock comes along and lightens the load with humor. Even though I don't understand why I am having this experience, I am reminded that even in the midst of pain, there are people whose presence is to be celebrated.

Mom and Aunt Doris and my nurse friend Brenda all came to visit today.

These amazing people help carry the burden, but at the end of the day, it is still up to me to do the work.

◦❦◦

I talked with Becca on the phone tonight. She said, "Mom, when you come home from the hospital, will you be a brand new mommy?"

Oh, I wish I could tell her "Yes." I wish I could say, "Becca, I will play with you. I will run and swim and bike with you." But

I can't.

Kelly was here yesterday. She thinks I need to look into having some medication for depression. I don't want to do it. I feel like a failure because I can't get through this on my own. There's a damn stubborn part of me that won't let me call anyone when I should. I think people are tired of listening to me. I need someone to help motivate me to get out of bed and move.

Friday, June 30th, Day 151

Sherlock came in this morning with the results of my fat test. The normal amount of fat to be found in the stool is about 7 grams, and my fat study had 97 grams. It means I am not absorbing anything. Bile salts to dissolve those fats are stored in the gallbladder, which would come in handy about now.

❧

Sherlock did an endoscopy today to see if my ileum is inflamed, but it looks healthy and pink. My stomach and duodenum, on the other hand, are very inflamed, so I will start taking Sandostatin to cut down the amount of stomach acid my body produces. It burns going into my arm, so the nurses will give it to me by IV. I wondered what will happen when I go home, and I may have to go back to using a central line for all my medications.

Sherlock asked me if I remembered anything about the endoscopy. I responded, "No, why?"

He replied, "Because you didn't like having that tube stuck down your throat. You hit me!"

I told him I was sorry. He said, "No, that's OK. Those things happen." Sherlock told me it was quite normal to cry under sedation, and hitting him was probably my attempt to release all the pent-up emotions. He thinks I should consider taking antidepressant medication, because I am crying more often than not when he comes into my room.

Sunday, July 2nd, Day 153

Mom called tonight from Omaha. She was at the family golf tournament, which has been going on for almost 25 years with her ten brothers and sisters. Along with golfing, everyone makes crafts, which are purchased at the picnic. This year, all the profits are coming to Tony and me. I'm overwhelmed with the love my aunts, uncles, and cousins have for me.

Sometimes I want to give up, but the love of many people keeps me going. Love is the only thing that carries me through some days.

To My Family and Friends

I have heard it said that the most difficult part of climbing Mt. Everest is not reaching the summit, but having the strength to make it safely back down the mountain to Base Camp.

Earlier this year, I received a very special gift from two climbers who had been on three expeditions to Mt. Everest, and who had both reached the summit. I received a Tibetan silk scarf called a "khata," which is a gift given to all climbers by the Sherpas, the mountain people of Nepal who accompany most expeditions to the mountain. Knowing that it has almost been to the top of the world has great meaning for me. They also sent me a postcard with a very encouraging message.

Jan, although we have never met, we understand you have climbed and survived a very dangerous mountain of late. You have faced death and overcome it. We send you sincere congratulations and hope for continued strength, determination, and courage. Signed, Jamie Clarke and Alan Hobson.

In their speaking presentations and books, Jamie and Alan tell the story of their teammate who got within two city blocks of the top before turning around due to high altitude sickness. He radioed to Base Camp and told his team that he could reach the summit but if he did, he would likely perish on the descent. The summit was not worth losing a life, so his team launched a high altitude rescue. They also began to talk him down the mountain via radio. He was exhausted and was climbing without the use of bottled oxygen, so for each step he took, he had to rest. Eventually he had to crawl. If it hadn't been for the radio contact with Base Camp, he never would have made it down the mountain. At one point, Base Camp connected the climber to his wife and daughters (ages 6 and 9) in Canada, and it was their voices that pulled him out of the snow and gave him the strength to keep moving. When he finally made it back to the team's high camp, his teammates were ready to receive him. During the rescue he lost consciousness and his breathing became shallow and erratic, but his teammates continued with the rescue anyway. It took them 33 continuous hours to get him down the mountain, but they saved his life. The radio had been his lifeline, and he credits his survival to his teammates and family, without whose help he might never have gotten back alive.

I, too, am trying to climb over a challenging mountain. As I struggle to take steps forward, the blowing snow knocks me down. I will only succeed with the strength, determination, and courage I receive from the countless prayers that continue to lift me up and keep me moving. My family and friends are the community; the team that maintains the vital communication that lets me know I am not alone. Your prayers, intentions, and good deeds are my radio, my lifeline. Without your help, I would be lost on a very cold and dark mountain.

There are times I wonder if I will ever get back to Base Camp. But, as Tony says, "Someday you will, Sweetheart. How can you not with all those radios out there?!"

Thank you for your love, your commitment, and prayers!

Monday, July 3rd, Day 154

I'm in better spirits today, maybe because I feel God's presence in my life through the people around me who come to comfort me and let me know they are still all praying. I am continually amazed at the love that is outpouring and coming my way.

I told Dr. M this morning that they weren't able to get a PICC line in, and he said, "Oh Jan, I remember when you first came into the emergency room after Sarah's birth. There were about 20 hospital staff standing around, and it took about a dozen times before they were able to get a central line in you. It was finally Dr. O who was able to do it. We were so nervous because you have to hit the subclavian vein right under the clavicle and right next to that is your lung. If they missed the vein, they could have punctured the lung. You would not have survived with a collapsed lung. I was very nervous watching them do the procedure." Hearing these kinds of stories is surreal for me.

Tuesday, July 4th, Day 155

Dr. M was just here with his wife and three girls. They were all going for a hike today before watching the fireworks. Oh, what I would give to hike with my kids! It's a beautiful day for a hike.

❧

Dr. M came in later by himself and asked me if I had reconsidered depression medication. I am not ready for it yet.

The nurses are going to pump me full of fluids since I only weigh 120 today. Then, this afternoon, they are going to give me a drug which will slow down the movement of the smooth muscles, hoping to slow down the action in my intestines. Because my heart is also a smooth muscle, my blood pressure will drop. The drug is in patch form, so if I get too dizzy, we will just take it off. I wonder how many experiments I have been a part of since the beginning of the year.

Family Time

Oohs and ahs
come from the crowd
of small bodies
gathered on the hospital bed.

Color drips from the sky
in reds and blues,
and snakes of white
twirl around themselves
chasing their tails.
Yellow, purple,
green and orange,
explode into lighted sprays
that charge the night.

Watching fireworks
with Mom is the best treat.

Well,
besides riding endlessly
up and down
on her hospital bed.
giggling.

Not a normal Fourth of July,
yet memory making
just the same.

Wednesday, July 5th, Day 156

Sherlock called the "diarrhea gurus" in Dallas, and he told two separate doctors my story. Both of them agreed that my gastrin level in the stomach is something to be concerned about. So, the next plan is to put in a central line and start me on TPN. Then, a nasogastric tube will be inserted for two days, so they can measure the levels of gastrin. Gastrin stimulates the cells in the stomach to secrete hydrochloric acid, which the doctors think is causing the excess fluid. Once the test is complete, the doctors will know how much medication to send through an IV. Any medication taken by mouth is being flushed out with all the extra output.

When I go home, I will be on TPN at night and can eat for pleasure during the day. The doctors agreed that this is why my fistula is not healing—that there is just too much stuff running through it. Hopefully, we will be able to see a change in the fistula. I want this to be the answer. Right now, I am not dealing well with all the mysteries of my body.

Sherlock said, "By the way, your dinner wasn't very good. I had to eat it, because I won't be home until late tonight, and I just wanted you to know you didn't miss much!"

I smiled. "Thanks!"

I'm glad Sherlock is on my case. I know he is just as frustrated as I am. I did tell him that I might be ready to use an antidepressant, but he can't give me oral drugs until we are finished with this test on Friday.

Sherlock asked me why I was recording my thoughts. I joked, "It's so that when you leave I can record how mean you are and complain about the terrible tests you are putting me through!"

Sherlock flapped back sarcastically, "Yeah, he doesn't care about you at all!" I know that's not true. Sometimes, I think he cares too much. He did tell me that often doctors get angry about not finding answers and they take it out on their patients. "You are much too nice to get angry at," he said.

Sherlock and Dr. M have put a lot of time into helping me get well. Sherlock recently defended me against the two doctors in Dallas who said, "Are you sure she's not just taking a bunch of laxatives?"

As if I have nothing better to do than take laxatives so I can spend time in a hospital! Sherlock jokingly said, "I know you have your stash in the top drawer over there, right?"

"Yeah," I quipped, laughing at the joke. My tiny sense of humor can get me through some tough days.

OLD BELIEFS DIE HARD. THERE WAS A BIGGER MONSTER gripping me—bigger than the depression itself. Her name was Perfectionism. For some reason, I felt if I took an anti-depressant, I was a failure. It meant I was not strong enough to handle the stress of my life by myself, and I would be judged as weak. In fact, the only person judging me was me. I remembered how well Perfectionism and Judgment play together. I never did give in. I never allowed myself the break an anti-depressant might have given me—a little space in which to think. I may have been able to deal with my illness in a more even-keeled manner. However, due to my old thinking, an anti-depressant was admitting defeat. To me, if felt like I was letting the illness win—and I wasn't about to let that happen.

There are days when I stare Perfectionism in the face, and she won't back down. I feel like I should be better, faster at my learning curve, too old to make the same mistakes. Perfectionism shows up in my life as "shoulds," bringing Judgment along with her. I fall short of my own expectations on a regular basis. Tony reminds me that life is about the journey, not the destination. Sometimes I am too caught up in where I think I should be to appreciate how far I have come, how much I have already accomplished. Turning my "shoulds" into "coulds" allows me the space to make the best decisions for me. Awareness of my language is the first step toward change.

In the last days of writing this book, I found myself unable to finish the final pages. When I paused to reflect on where I was, I realized the only voice I was listening to was Perfectionism. She was loud, sharing her fear about the book not being perfect. She was afraid and worried people might not like my book.

I wanted to be rid of her. I wanted her voice to quit ringing in my ears, coloring everything I wrote. I even dreamt that my husband had killed the person I know as Perfectionism. And while I thought that would make me feel better, an ache in my heart helped me realize that attacking her with anger and banning her from my life was not the answer. Whether I was willing to acknowledge her or not, she had played a major role in my survival over the years. Yelling at her only made her dig in her heels all the more, drowning out the voices of Wisdom and Compassion within me.

Across the pages of my journal, I wrote to her and asked her to express her fears. I treated her with kindness, and slowly, her voice quieted. Other voices spoke up, encouraging me, reminding me that I am a good writer, and that my story will touch the lives of those who will listen. And while this book won't be perfect, it will be my story, told in truth to the best of my ability in this present moment.

> If we begin to get in touch with whatever we feel with some kind of kindness, our protective shells will melt, and we'll find that more areas of our lives are workable.
> - Pema Chodron, *When Things Fall Apart*

I don't want Perfectionism to leave. When she gets excited, it is my job to become quiet and allow the other voices of Love and Wisdom to speak louder, reminding me that who I am is enough.

In those moments when I feel most at peace, I realize that peace comes from acceptance and the willingness to sit with both my gifts and my limitations. I cannot hide the dark parts of myself. If I want to live an authentic life, I have to allow my humanity to shine through all the experiences of my life. Pretending I am perfect doesn't serve me or others. Allowing others to see the real me, with the good and rough parts, gives permission to others to be authentic in their own lives. And that brings healing to a world in need of more love.

Thursday, July 6th, Day 157

I now have an NG tube in place. I am sore from the foreign intruder up my nose and clogging the back of my throat. How did I manage with this tube for all the time I was in ICU? I didn't. I remember pulling it out and having the nurses quickly respond by tying down my arms and replacing it. In a semi-comatose state, I was operating in a different realm. I thought at the time that I was pulling it out of my eye. Did I feel like a lab rat, being poked and prodded with every imaginable tube? I still feel that way today. Each movement of my head brings me back to the presence of a plastic tube sticking out of my nose. The physical pain of moving is doubled by the emotional and mental pain of not being in control of my body. I wonder where I will find the answers to getting well. It hurts to talk. I don't know if this tube will help or not, but since I can't do anything about it, I will try to sleep.

Friday, July 7th, Day 158

Freedom! The NG tube is out!

I've had two shots of morphine today because of pain from a new central line. Morphine makes my body feel weird, so I will ask for Tylenol. I am sure the emotional pain of cutting and pasting a third ileostomy seal doesn't help.

We pulled the tube from the fistula. Sherlock thinks it's the only way it's going to heal and we might as well "go for it." I will now be on TPN for 14 hours at night. I am working with a new mantra: *My body is going to heal. My body is going to heal.*

I had many visitors today. My mom's friend Sharon came down from Fort Collins and did healing touch for an hour. Being quiet and calm allowed me to recognize that God has surrounded me with friends and family who love me and support me and hospital staff that want to see me get well. I know my doctors are doing everything they can to get me out of here.

Sunday, July 9th, Day 160

My nurse friend Brenda rescued me from the hospital tonight to attend a concert in which Tony was singing. I was afraid the doctors wouldn't let me go, because I had no measurable blood pressure when I stood up, but somehow I convinced them that it was important to me and I was in the hands of an ICU nurse, so I would be OK. I wasn't planning on standing anyway! Brenda was awesome to take that responsibility.

A Song of Love
Kathy McGovern, Member of Ekklesia

I remember the night Tony was a guest artist with Ekklesia. It was a pleasure to have him sing with us, but we were apprehensive that he might not be able to perform because of the devastating illness of his wife. We had all heard about her horrific journey to the doors of death, but I wasn't prepared for the tiny, fragile, doll-like young woman whom Tony introduced to the audience. I remember his words clearly:

I am so happy tonight because my beautiful wife Jan is here. She has suffered an unbelievable ordeal for the past six months, but she's alive and she is here with me. She's the love of my life.

And of course none of us could sing a note as our hearts filled with love for them both. The audience clapped and clapped for a woman they didn't know, but who was loved so deeply by this talented troubadour. It was a long time ago, but the love in Tony's voice still echoes through the years.

Monday, July 10th, Day 161

Dr. M has ordered extra fluids to be added to my TPN to

help me stay hydrated, especially in the hot weather. I'm going to be watching my "ins" and "outs" and will have to monitor my blood sugar at home because of the extra glucose in the TPN. A home health nurse twice a day will help me learn the new medical routine. I will try not to eat anything and just let the TPN do its work. Maybe the fistula can start to heal now that the feeding tube is out.

Tony bought me some Depends to help me with my drainage. There are some that can be put right into my panties, and we will see if that can catch the drips from the wound because everything I drink goes right through me. This morning, I was changing my dressing every 45 minutes, and I can't do that for long periods of time.

I have noticed little improvements in my health since I have been in the hospital. I walk several times a day and now have a 70-degree bend in my knee. I expect that to improve when my walking increases at home. I am getting around much more quickly on my crutches and even get up at night by holding on to the IV pole and pushing it to the bathroom. The little successes get lost in the overall scheme of things, yet I have to remember that each baby step gets me closer to being well.

Even though this has been a detour on my journey, and I don't have any answers, I am learning to understand the abnormalities of my body better. It is time to go home and be with my girls.

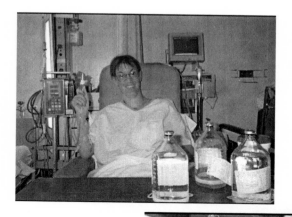

(Above) My Last Day in ICU, (Right) Touring the New Floor, (Below) Standing On My Own, Stacking Cones

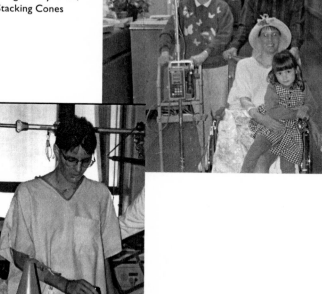

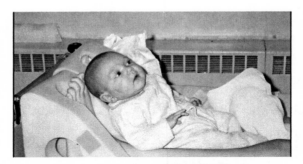

(Top) A Unique Way of Holding Sarah, (Middle) The Girls
and Tony Ready for Easter, (Below) Three Little Angels

(Above) Standing with Tony and Mary Beth, (Right) My First Look at Home in 76 Days! (Below) Learning to Walk with One Crutch

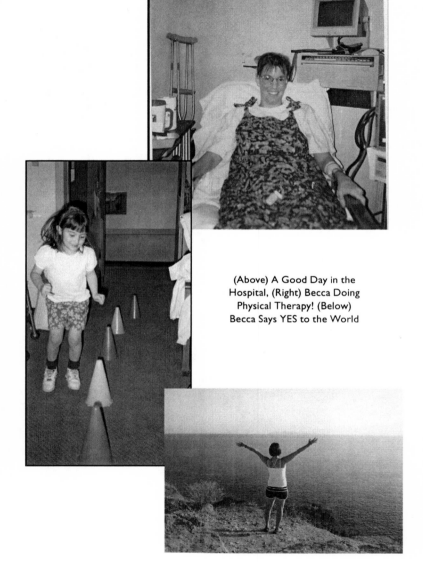

(Above) A Good Day in the Hospital, (Right) Becca Doing Physical Therapy! (Below) Becca Says YES to the World

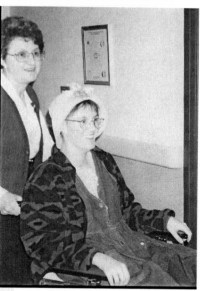

(Above) Going Home Celebration-Day 100! (Right) Mom and I Leave the Hospital—Freedom after 100 Days! (Below) Note In My Guest Book From My Cousin Lori

Jan—

Wow! 100 long, arduous days behind you! Way to go! No matter how hard + painful the coming months are— just remember how far you've come! We have witnessed a true miracle in your recovery!

lve + prayers—
Lori + Steve

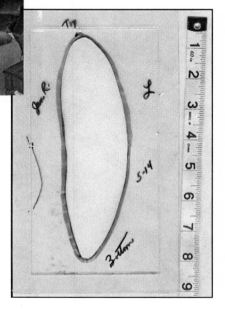

(Above) A Celebration Meal for Coming Home! (Left) Welcomed Home with Love and Hugs From Becca (Below) The Size of My Wound When I Got Home

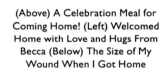

(Above) Hannah and I Fall Asleep in the Care of Each Other
(Right) Discovering the Love of Sarah
(Below) The Daily Physical Therapy

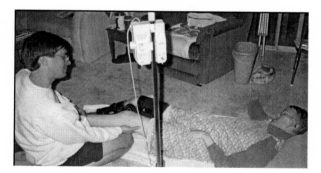

(Above) Out for my Daily Walk, (Left) Kelly Gaul Visits and Helps Me Process My Journey (Below) Riding Up and Down on the Bed with Uncle Dave

The Long Haul

*Difficult things take a long time,
impossible things a little longer.*

André A. Jackson

Home Again

IT WAS A DINNER PARTY AT MARY BETH AND JEFF'S HOUSE in the late summer the year following my illness. Tony's sister and brother-in-law have always been active people, even taking a bike trip for their honeymoon. So, it was no surprise the people invited to dinner were friends who were all physically active. Conversations revolved around training for marathons, competing in triathlons, climbing Colorado Fourteeners, mountain biking, and so on. As people were sharing their tales of athletic feats, one woman turned to me and said, "So what do you do?"

I replied, "I spent part of my life in a hospital last year. I walk, and that is a great accomplishment."

Mary Beth caught my eye, smiled and said, "Yes, she is right. Walking is a good thing!"

Thursday, July 13th, Day 164

I'm lying on the bed at home changing a dressing while everyone else is out in the kitchen eating. They don't wait for me since food is not one of my pleasures these days. I feel invisible in my own home. I can engage myself in the conversation and be a part of their lives, yet even the conversation around the table is about food, especially when dealing with young children. "Eat three more bites. If you eat your broccoli you can have dessert." I will have to get out of this funk.

I had an appointment with Sherlock yesterday. Basically, he told me I'm going to be on TPN (IV nutrition) until the fistula heals. My prayers have become more fervent that the fistula heals quickly, although the underlying anger at feeling stuck is ever present. Dr. M called and said," I'm going through Jan Haas withdrawals! I haven't seen you for three days." I thought it was pretty funny. I didn't get to walk today. We just changed the ileostomy bag for the fourth time. It gets very old having the seal break, and I don't know how to do anything differently to make it stay.

It is hard to admit that many times as a busy mom, dinner at our house has consisted of a bowl of cereal, or maybe apples, peanut butter, a bowl of popcorn, and a good movie. We are definitely not fancy meal people, and while we like to eat healthy and fresh, most meals I cook can be made in a stir-fry pan or on the grill in less than 30 minutes. Time spent sharing our day at the dinner table is our focus.

When I was sick and often unable to eat, each meal I denied myself seemed like a seven-course meal prepared by a chef. I am reminded of the scene from the movie *Chocolat*, when the chocolatier in town makes a birthday dinner for an odd assortment of friends. As the guests partake of the rich food—succulent roasted turkey smothered in a chocolate mole sauce—their eyes close to take in the taste of something wonderful. They lick their lips of the sweetness of life and laugh at the conversation that nourishes body and soul. I felt as if I was missing that kind of meal each time I sat at the table, unable to eat even a bowl of cereal.

To eat or not to eat became the question. With IV nutrition, TPN, giving me all the nutrients I needed, eating was an on again-off again experience. At first, the doctors were convinced that eating would slow down the healing process.

When I was not able to eat, I excluded myself from the social part of our family life. It was incredibly difficult to share meal times when no food could pass my lips. Sitting at the dinner table, I had to learn to feast on the conversation and the people who were present, rather than the food placed before everyone else.

Not eating would have been easier if there had been a strong connection to real results—a decrease in the gastric juices pouring from my wound and ileostomy. Yet, this theory didn't hold true. Sometimes, I would go for weeks without eating, hoping the wound would heal. At first, it seemed to worked, with maybe four dressing changes a day. And then I would have five days when I changed the dressing ten times each day, without rhyme or reason. I would wonder why I was denying myself, call the doctor, and go back to eating again.

The loss of so many things made not eating that much more difficult. I was already functioning in a place way out of my comfort zone, so eating was a comfort—both from the familiar taste sensation and the social aspect of sharing an event with my family.

Saturday, July 15th, Day 166

This morning, Tony and I went to Kazoo and Company on a shopping trip to buy Becca a birthday present. I have been "cooped up" for so long that taking a trip felt good. We were gone for three hours, and even though my dressing was soaked, it wasn't leaking all over the place. Things are looking up. Another mantra: *This wound is going to heal. Thank you, God. This wound is going to heal. Thank you, God.*

Monday, July 17th, Day 168

The disability has been approved—a check will be coming soon.

Wednesday, July 19th, Day 170

Yesterday, I went to Washington Park with the girls and watched them play. If I really want to get better, I have to be active and leave the house. It's more exciting to go somewhere than it is to walk up and down the street. The wound is actually closing from both ends. Even though it is deep, it shrunk from 14 cm to 12 cm in one week.

Thursday, July 20th, Day 171

Yesterday, Aunt Doris drove me to Fort Collins to visit Mom. I wore a skirt and t-shirt and this crazy denim hat I wear to cover my bald head. Real clothes! I even put on a little makeup! Sharon and her friend Katherine blessed with me a healing touch session. During the hour they worked on me, Sharon asked me to imagine colors, as in a rainbow. The colors I had the most difficult time imagining were orange and yellow. Those colors represent the energy centers, or chakras, in my abdomen where the wound is. Although I am skeptical about what I can't see and understand, I have faith that any work on my body can help me heal.

I am working with a new visualization: I sit on the beach and let salt water pour over my body as the waves come in. I watch the salt dry up my fistula and heal it. I see the wound get smaller and disappear. The water also hits my knee and wears away the calcium deposit.

My knee bends up to 74 degrees today, a sign that it continues to get better.

Aunt Doris

Through a broken and sobbing voice,
she hears the need and answers the call.
In no time, she is standing in the doorway
to my bedroom.

"What's up?' she says.
Words spew out of me like
bile pouring out of a fistula.
Angry, foul negativity I can no longer contain.

"What else?" she inquires.
Excuses spill forth—
too tired, bad night, achy body,

raw skin, dressing changes,
too much crap for my mind to filter.

"Are you done?" she asks.
The sign my complaining must stop.

"I just want this to all go away,"
is my last feeble attempt
at rousing the sympathies
of the tough-love coach.

"Well, it won't, so it is time to get up. NOW!"

On my feet, away from my solo pity party,
and into the shower
where I cry my remaining tears of frustration
and strengthen my resolve.

Then I am dressed and out the door,
counting steps
so as not to fall short of
yesterday's accomplishment
and to make tomorrow's win
that much sweeter.

"So, what's good in your life, Jan?"
The answers come so clearly now.
My Positive Mental Attitude Coach
is working her magic.
"People who love and care about me,
people who won't let me give up.
Three little girls to fight for,
A life with Tony.

I can walk and move and talk and see and hear."

"And?"
"I am alive!" I say,
surprising myself with the truth.

"Yes, you are," she softens.
"So make us proud—
The only thing you can do
is what is before you—
Get well."

No more pity parties, no more lying around,
extra effort in all I do,
grateful for being alive...
until the phone call the next week
when my PMA coach is beckoned again.

Mom's Journal,
Friday, July 21st, Day 172

This morning Dr. L, a doctor I work with, asked me how Jan was, so I updated him. From a medical point of view, of course, she still has many hurdles to overcome. I told him that we were thankful she wasn't mentally disabled in some way, which she surely could have been—we were blessed by the fact that she can enjoy her girls and appreciate and interact with friends. Dr. L told me I was always looking for the good things. Well! Let me tell you—that isn't easy. It is far easier to fall into the trap of looking at what isn't right, all the problems Jan continues to face, minute by minute, hour after hour. But God is good. We praise and thank Him daily for giving Jan back to us. We believe that He will heal her and that out of this nightmare, good things will happen. We thank Him for Tony who has been such a "rock" and faithful support for her and their beautiful girls. God has a special purpose in mind for Jan and her family. We don't know what it is, but we know there is one.

A friend called today to see how I was doing. Caring friends are so supportive. Today, though, I find myself fighting back tears when I talk about Jan. I guess it's just "one of those days," and it will pass like all the rest.

Tuesday, July 25th, Day 176

My knee braces are retiring to the garage! I am using a cane right now, but I don't want to put the crutches in the garage just yet. They are my safety blanket. Yesterday, I bent my leg 75 degrees, compared to last Thursday when I could only bend it 72 degrees. Progress comes, one degree at a time.

I believe the fistula is healing. I pray that it is healing. I'm trying to visualize the sun. Yellow is the color of the solar plexus chakra, right where my stomach is, so I am using visualization to heal my body.

Thursday, July 27th, Day 178

I laughed and cried today as I reread cards I have received from the community around me. There are so many that I had to find a bigger box to hold them. I am overwhelmed by the number of people who continue to support us through this long ordeal.

Thursday, August 3th, Day 185

My ileostomy bag came off again. It is frustrating when the seal doesn't last more than a day. The wound is leaking so much I have to change the dressings every two hours, and the skin is raw.

A yeast infection all over the skin makes it painful to touch. It is easy to forget my blessings when all hell breaks loose.

I went to Fort Collins, and my mom's friend Connie tried to teach me how to put an ostomy bag on the wound. That would mean instead of dressings, I would have two bags to empty. If we can find the right materials to make it work, it may be the solution I am looking for.

Saturday, August 5th, Day 187

My brother Jim and his wife, Paula, came over tonight to help celebrate Becca's birthday. I spent time in the kitchen baking Becca's birthday cake, and I threw together a potato casserole. I have been doing my best to keep a positive attitude.

The skin is wasting away under all the caustic juices from the fistula. It hurts constantly. I try to visualize this fistula closing. I want it to be closed NOW!

I return to my mantra: *This fistula will close. This fistula will close.*

Many times, the only way to get through these days is to just rest in the mother arms of God. Thank goodness they are big enough to hold me.

Tuesday, August 8th, Day 190

There are days when the weight of this illness prevents me from picking up a tiny tape recorder capable of lessoning my burden. I am paralyzed by the continued trauma, and even talking becomes impossible.

I went to see Sherlock last Tuesday. I may have celiac-sprue, an autoimmune disease which makes me allergic to wheat, rye and barley. Another test will show if I have the antibody for it, and then we will know for sure. The disease can be brought on by acute illness.

In the larger scope of things, having celiac disease is not the end of the world. I am alive. But just when I am starting to eat again, I now have to worry about what kinds of foods I can eat. I never realized that wheat is in everything!

At times, I feel I am in a B-grade movie that just won't stop. I am looking around for the next catastrophe to hit. I have been at this for six-and-a-half long months, and it seems like years. I am tired after an hour of activity and can't imagine going back to work anytime soon. Healing is my work.

Here's an excerpt from the letter I just got done writing to my friend Sue in Cedar Rapids.

> ...The fistula hasn't healed, and my skin has a rash from the drainage. I change the dressing too frequently, seven or eight times a day. In the hospital I used to say, "If only I didn't have a fistula, I'd be so much better." Now, I just survive each day, doing what needs to get done. No matter how frustrated I get, I still have to change dressings. All my wishing doesn't make the problems go away. My patience is tested daily, as is my faith and endurance. I often find myself reminding God not to give me more than we can handle.
>
> On the bright side, my knee now has a 78-degree bend, and I am active in the house. I only use the cane when I go outside. In July, Tony and I went to a Rockies baseball game, and for Becca's birthday on Sunday, we went to see the movie "Pocahontas." I am gaining some sense of normalcy by helping with home chores.
>
> I am on IV nutrition, TPN, 14 hours a day, which runs at night. I give myself a saline IV every day to keep hydrated. I can do these routines without a thought, now that I am quite adept at taking

*care of my medical needs. Keeping the central line clean and
hooking up to IV is second nature to me.*

*Tony is taking me driving soon to see if I can brake with my left
foot. Then, I can start doing outpatient physical therapy.*

Keep the cards coming. They make a world of difference.

Tuesday, August 15th, Day 197

I talked to Sherlock yesterday. My body is starting to make
blood again, a good sign that I am healing. But the mystery isn't
solved. The tests are inconclusive on celiac disease. Now, I don't
know why I had excessive diarrhea in the hospital. As much as I
hoped we had an answer, I am glad to get to eat whatever I want.
What a roller coaster ride!

Friday, August 18th, Day 200

Yesterday, I went to see Dr. P, hoping he would be willing
to operate on the fistula. Of course, he's not ready. He would
rather I heal on my own than risk more problems with surgery.
The walls of the intestine are pretty thin. However, he is willing
to stitch the top of the fistula closed and try to pull the skin over
it so that it heals on its own. It will be outpatient surgery with a
local anesthetic. At least there is forward motion.

Hannah came home from school, I was cutting Kerlix, the
gauze I used to redress the wound, and she said, "Mom, you all
better?"

I said "No, not yet Hannah."

She looked at me with her two-and-a-half-year-old silliness,
"I'm going to buy you a new tummy. Here it is, on my ear. Are
you ready?" She took it off her ear, and she threw it at me, wanting
me to catch it.

Her silliness brought light to the moment. I too am looking forward to the day when my tummy doesn't "run" anymore.

Hannah Magic

FROM THE MOMENT HANNAH WAS BORN, AND I LOOKED into her eyes, I knew a wise person had taken residence in this baby. At five pounds ten ounces, Hannah was a tiny baby, but what she lacked in size, Hannah more than made up for in personality. We moved to Colorado when Hannah was eight months old, at a time when she decided that baby food and being fed by mom or dad was not what she wanted. She wanted to feed herself, so she lived on the vegetables in canned soup until she could finally wield the spoon that flung food to all parts of the kitchen. When I was pregnant with Sarah, I was the favored parent. Tony was greeted each morning by a grunt and a call for "Mama," so I helped Hannah get ready for the day. It was this same Hannah who held my hand in the hospital and whispered "I love you Mommy" over and over again until I thought my heart would burst.

At two-and-a-half, Hannah sat on my bed and, as if it was natural to have a mom with a hole in her abdomen, she would help me cut the gauze to dress my wound. I can see her as if it were yesterday, hair pulled back in a half ponytail with a pink ribbon, a neon-green, polka dot dress, her tennis shoes tucked underneath her. Her wise eyes danced with ideas, and just maybe she could create a new tummy out of thin air. Maybe life's mysteries would play into her hand and give her the winning card.

Over the years, Hannah fell in love with the mystery of life, and believed whole-heartedly in things unseen. Inspired to search for leprechauns at the MPB Early Learning Center, Hannah crafted traps out of shiny paper, fake gold coins, and shoe boxes, determined to catch one and make it her own. You can imagine her dismay when the crafty tooth fairy left a note, revealing that while delivering money for a tooth, he heard a racket in the kitchen, took pity on a trapped leprechaun, and released him. For years after, Hannah and the leprechaun had an ongoing battle with bigger and better traps and glitter sprawled across the kitchen floor saying, "Ha ha, you can't catch me!" From leprechaun traps to fairy houses under the spruce tree, Hannah operated under the assumption that just because you can't see something, doesn't mean it doesn't exist.

Maybe that day, I needed some of Hannah's magic. I wanted her to sprinkle her fairy-dust belief in the goodness of life over my belly and magically make it heal. And while that didn't happen, the magic of Hannah's love did work its magic on my soul, helping me to more readily accept the mystery of life.

Sadly, the call for "Mama" went away as Hannah got older. I felt her pain as she moved through junior high, following the ups and downs of most teenagers. The umbilical cord stretched as she turned 18 and readied herself for college. When we were leaving her in

Minnesota for her freshman year, the words, "Mama, I
love you" tumbled out of her mouth. My heart danced, as
once again, I was captured in Hannah's magic.

Wednesday, August 23rd, Day 205

My outpatient surgery with Dr. P. went well. It is 24 hours
later, and the stitches are still intact. While I was under anesthetic,
I received a new central line. The old one was starting to beep
at me, meaning my TPN wasn't flowing well. Tonight, Hannah
wanted to lay with me, and I had to tell her to be very careful
because she kept bumping my stomach and my shoulder where
the central line stiches are. I am tired and in pain. My frustration
level has increased because I can't snuggle and feel the comfort of
my children.

God, please hear my prayer. Help this fistula to stay closed,
to not leak, and to bring me some peace of mind. Just a little
peace and healing.

Hannah said she would buy me a new tummy for Christmas.
I hope I don't have to wait that long.

Tuesday, August 29th, Day 211

I'm on my fourth liter of IV fluids to build back up the
hydration I've lost. I can't keep losing and taking in five liters a
day of fluid. At least I'm here and not in the hospital.

Wednesday, September 6th, Day 219

The stitches in my belly lasted for 11 days, but they broke
when we were up at the cabin in Grand Lake. The supplies we
had weren't enough for the output, so Tony had to go into town

and buy all the gauze he could find.

At yesterday's appointment with Dr. P, he opened the door without even saying hi or hello and said, "Did you hear the one about the blonde who went to the dentist?" His eccentric personality and ability to crack jokes when a situation is tense is one of his endearing qualities. It helps make up for his typical surgeon's bedside manner. It was obvious that the stitches did not hold and they wouldn't hold for long the next time, but the pain on my face told him that more stitches were necessary to hold my life together.

Regardless of what happens, I am glad I am alive. My children are the most precious gifts, and I get to enjoy them every single day. I'm very lucky to be here. I just wonder what all of this means in my life.

WHEN A PERSON IS STRESSED AT WORK, OFTEN HE OR SHE can leave work and take a walk outside, and hopefully, the fresh air can bring about a new perspective. They can exercise and renew their energy. When it is the body that is stressed, there is no way to get away from the physical pain except in one's mind. I often retreated into my mind with visualization. I would allow the ocean to hold me and bathe me in healing waters, or I would go to a mountain top and allow the warmth of the sun to fill me and make me whole. There were times I used music to guide my visualizations, feeling the vibration of song moving my cells, believing that together the words and music could help. My favorite visualization was to lay myself in God's motherly arms. In a place of calm, I remembered that the suffering, the breaking of stitches, was just life happening to me, not God punishing me. I couldn't control what my body was doing, but I could decide to look for God. I knew that eventually God's love would shine through the pain, and I would be a stronger person having survived all the suffering.

Friday, September 8th, Day 221

Sherlock is still concerned about the drainage, so he is going to do a special test to see if my gastric levels are abnormal. He thinks I might have a gastric tumor that is producing an abundance of stomach acid.

Waking up each morning and recognizing I am in the same place gets harder each day. The desire to live outweighs the desire to give up, so I do what needs to be done. I have been through hell. At times I am still there. I have good moments and bad moments, and all I can do is live them one at a time. My girls need a mom. I am not going to be a victim of this illness. It's not in my nature. Someday, this will all be in the past.

I thank God for friends who continue to bless our lives, continue to create community, continue to give us bread, literally, to make us healthy and whole. The prayers keep pouring in.

During these days that I am not eating, it has been difficult to sit at the table and watch everyone else eat. Tony is trying to convince me that dinner is not just eating; it is social. Lately, I have been putting forth a better effort. I have done dishes and even helped cook. Imagine a cook in a kitchen not being able to taste test! Tony is right. Sharing a meal is a part of life. If I take myself out completely, I am missing life! I enjoy feeding Sarah, and I am helping Tony so he doesn't have to worry about her at meal times. There is something good about sitting at the table watching the girls, watching Tony interact with them, talking about our day, playing games. I have already missed so much. I don't want to miss this too.

I'll Take a Helping of Love

What's for dinner?
Pasta with pesto
and Becca telling kid jokes.
Giggles wrap around the kitchen
like spaghetti on a spoon.

What's for dinner?
Fresh sliced bread
and Hannah's tiny voice talking about big things.
My worries melt like butter.

What's for dinner?
Tossed salad with fresh herb dressing
and Sarah with her big brown eyes
and loud voice.
A medley of baby sounds mixing
with little girl chatter.

What's for dinner?
Cookies and ice cream
and Tony appreciating time with his girls,
savoring the sweetness of the moment.

What's for Dinner?
A ten-pound IV bag of TPN.
No spaghetti, no bread, no salad,
no cookies, no ice cream,
but a huge helping of Becca, Hannah, Sarah, and
Tony.

I am content.

Living Life Half-Assed

Saturday, September 9th, Day 222

Our gourmet group met today for brunch, and even though

> The only disability in life is a bad attitude.
>
> - Scott Hamilton

I couldn't eat, I sat at the table and talked to everyone, catching up with all my cousins. I enjoyed a short walk to Wash Park, where a croquet course was set up for a couple's game. We would hit every other shot. My cousin Jeff looked at me and asked, "Do you think you can play?"

I said, "You bet! I'm in there." Walking on the uneven grass was a challenge for me, but I wanted to play.

Two of the ladies just sat there. "I had a hard week," and "I'm tired, and I'm not going to play," were their replies when asked to join the fun.

Watching them sit on the sideline really burned me. I thought to myself, "She's got two perfectly good legs. She's got a perfectly good middle that doesn't have a hole in it. I don't understand why she can't enjoy life. It may not be something that really excites her, but we're out here to have fun with each other. Why exclude yourself?" I wonder how often I have chosen to not participate fully in life because I was too tired or I didn't feel like playing. How many times did I not play because I knew I couldn't be perfect at something? That's the lesson I am learning. I can't do everything, but I have to participate in the things I can do. You know the saying, "Don't do anything half-assed?" Well, right now, that is all I can do. So I say, even if I can only participate in life half-assed, it is better than watching life pass me by!

Friday, September 15th, Day 228

Tony has a 45-minute commute, by the time he picks up the girls and comes home. We are still getting meals from the wonderful volunteers from church. One night, it is grilled salmon. Another night, it might be chicken and roasted vegetables. I tell myself that someday I will be able to eat again.

My shoulder is sore from the placement of yet another new central line for my TPN feedings. The other line kept beeping, as if it were clogged or not in the right position. When I came out from under the effects of Versed in surgery, tears ran down my face and sobs shook my body. While there was a release of pent-up emotions, I am spent. Dr. P. stitched me up again, even though we both know this is not a permanent fix. Even two days without drainage helps soothe my skin.

One bright light in my day was when I pedaled all the way around on the bicycle at physical therapy. My knee now has a 105-degree bend.

Prayer is like work for me. A quote from Thomas Merton says, "True love and prayer are really learned in the hour when prayer becomes impossible and your heart turns to stone." Maybe not stone, but I am numb, worn down by so much trauma with no relief. Even still, through all the darkness, I know that God is with me. I don't blame God for my illness. God didn't create this situation just to make me suffer. I know God is with me in the midst of my suffering. I may not be saying my prayers, but I am truly living them. I want God to take away my pain, but deeper than that, I want to know I am not alone. I want to feel God holding me with motherly arms, whispering, "I am with you." My unspoken prayer speaks louder than I thought. A faith deep within has sustained me through this illness.

Prayer

My unspoken prayer rises like incense,
curling and swirling
its way to heaven.

Words only trap my prayer
in human constructs,
letters in formation,
a bird in a cage.

Yet beyond my ability to comprehend
the mystery of Love,
God holds an outstretched palm
and gathers to Her own breast
the wishes of my heart,
unspoken, unvoiced,
felt in every cell of my body.

In the silent exchange,

peace settles like snow,
calming my restless spirit.
Divine Wisdom answers with goodness
the prayers I don't even know to ask.

And while my human eyes may fail to see
at a soul level I know—
The God of Infinite Love
holds me in deep regard.
All shall be well.

Mission

Monday, September 18th, Day 231

I was well enough to participate in our parish mission week. Our presenter was very theatrical and full of energy.

On the first night, we were asked to share a bible story that had special meaning for us. Although I couldn't come up with one story, I definitely could relate to the Israelites crying out, "Where are you, God?" Many times this year, I felt alone on my journey.

In small groups, we were asked to share a time when we had to sacrifice something. Gee, I don't know. Do you think a whole year counts? Tony and I have had to make so many sacrifices. A friend told Tony that we have been the sacrificial lamb for Most Precious Blood Church.

I was thinking about sacrifice all the way home and about the crosses we bear. When we walked in the door, everyone took off their coat and Tony put down the diaper bag and Sarah's carrier and I pulled the IV bag off my shoulder. Everyone else was shedding their baggage, and it dawned on me that it's my cross to carry this bag of food for 14 hours each day. As much as I want to shed this year of my life, I am still buried under the weight of it. And yes, sometimes I fall and need someone to carry it for me, like Simon helped Jesus carry the cross. I am literally living that sacrifice, living with a cross every day.

Community feels like a warm blanket on a cold night, kind words, and a cup of hot chocolate. Last night, a couple that we had just met said, "You know Jan, your story has touched so many people.'"

Tony and I like to think of ourselves as ordinary people, who—given a set of circumstances—are just traveling along doing the best we can. I think anyone given this cross to bear would do their best too. I'm in awe of the deep faith that runs through me, allowing me to stay mostly positive in the midst of the pain. Apparently, people in our community think we are extraordinary, walking this path with grace. If it is grace we are walking with, it is because God's love continues to shine through all the darkness, showing us the way.

So, is this our mission then, to shine through the darkness and give others hope to live through the challenges they face? Tony and I agree this is a pivotal story in our lives. This is our resurrection story. This is our story of coming back to life from the depths of all evil or all bad or the lowest of the low. I had to ask Tony, "When will we rise?"

He said, "I don't know, Babe, but we will."

I know Jesus, in his human experience, walked this path of loneliness, of frustration, of anger, of fear, of "I don't want this cross anymore." And I know that Jesus will hold my hand and keep walking with me until I am able to rise to a brand-new life.

An Organized Plan
Adele Deline, family friend

Sixteen years after Jan's close brush with death, I marvel at how many people it took to aid in her recovery with God as the Master planner! I look back over the list of women in our community at Most Precious Blood Church who jumped in to do our small part to help Jan and her family. Prayer and the Spirit's guidance were our first priority. Devastated as we were, "yes" was the answer to the call for help. With the help of many, an organized plan to assist with cleaning or laundry and food came into being.

Is it a hidden code of God somewhere that one never gives without receiving? The months of planning and organizing volunteer schedules blessed us thirty fold with grace and friendship as we helped sustain this family. It was definitely a labor of love that touched all of our hearts.

Another aspect of this experience was working with Jan's husband, Tony. As we worked together on the Environmental Committee to enhance the worship space at church, I felt his quiet sense of helplessness dealing with his physical and emotional pain—father of a newborn and two toddlers, coach for his helpless wife, and maintaining his job as the Liturgist of Most Precious Blood Parish. There was always an unspoken prayer in our work and sharing.

Jan relives and tells her story for us all, and as I reflect again on her journey, tears flow. Jan has more to do and to become in this life, as mom, wife, mentor, co-leader, and much more. Today, we witness a miracle before us with gratitude and joy!

Epiphany Moment

NOT LONG AFTER MISSION WEEK AT CHURCH, I WAS HAVING another rough day. Visualizing my body in the arms of Mother God was a comfort, and it allowed me to relax. Although I had visualized these arms of safety many times, today I felt a need to see God's face, to look into the eyes of God. In my mind's eye, I looked up from my resting place and saw all the people who had carried us through the year—the people who brought food and diapers, the people who cleaned and visited me, the family and friends who loved me. These were the workers who were helping me move the mountain of illness. God was so very present in my life, in the very people who prayed and worked for my journey back to health.

In that moment, a blanket of love surrounded me, so thick and warm I knew beyond a shadow of a doubt that I would survive this journey. I knew that my suffering was not just for me and that my story could bring hope to others. In that moment, all of me was at peace.

Putting the Pieces Together

Tuesday, September 19th, Day 232

Last night, I dreamt I drove Tony to a store in the van. The rundown store was in the poorest part of town. When we got there, the only other car in the parking lot was an old, beat-up junker a gang was stripping for parts. Before entering the store, Tony gave me a knife and said, "Here, wait for me. I will be back."

I stared at him with big eyes and cried, "I don't want to stay here."

He replied, "You have no choice."

I was left alone to defend myself. As soon as Tony went

inside, the gang members came up and started attacking the van. I couldn't get away. The keys might have been in the ignition, but for some reason, I didn't think to drive the van even around the block. I was paralyzed, and I didn't want to leave Tony. So, I used the knife to protect myself.

❧

Today when Kelly came, she asked if I had been dreaming. When I told her about the dream, she had an insight to share. She thought, "The *worst part of town* might be symbolic of where you've been, in the lowest part of your life, and maybe the old, stripped-down car was your body. You were stripped of your old self and there was nothing you could do about it. The van represents your new self, and you are going to do everything you can to defend it. Maybe you are fighting the evils of your body you don't understand."

This interpretation made sense to me. I wanted to drive away, but obviously I can't get away from my body. Maybe I'm just learning to feel empowered, building belief in myself again.

It is time to call my doctors and ask for a solution. It is time to be more forceful, asserting myself to defend the only body I have.

Saturday, September 23rd, Day 236

Results are in. No gastric tumor, no overgrowth of bacteria, and no explanation for the overabundance of drainage. Sherlock is doing another endoscopy to see if I still have an inflamed small intestine. He is specifically looking at the health of the cilium— the finger-like projections in the intestine that help absorb nutrients. Anti-inflammatory medication given to people with Celiac disease might help solve my drainage problem. I may need to change my diet again. I am surprised these doctors haven't given up on me!

Dr. P is throwing his hands up too. He doesn't want to go into surgery because he is afraid of taking too much of my intestines. Both doctors want to do the right thing. I'm glad they're being cautious, although it does nothing for my frustration level.

Tuesday, September 26th, Day 239

Before the endoscopy, Sherlock said, "I'm going to heavily sedate you."

I said, "Why, because you don't want me to hit you?"

He replied, "That's exactly right!"

I reminded Sherlock that the last time I had Versed, I came out pretty teary. He said it was understandable and would probably happen again. "There are good reasons for doing the tests. Hopefully, the tears will be cleansing for you."

Dr. Sherlock Holmes

Not an extremely tall man
yet a presence nonetheless
in his suit jacket
and professional manner.

His stethoscope his pipe,
a sleuthing tool for figuring out
the unknown.
His brow wrinkles in thought
and I imagine files upon files
organizing in his head

as he puts the pieces of me,
the puzzle,
together.

Yet, as the puzzle I am,
Sherlock is never the scientist
regarding me a specimen,
nor the egotistical doctor
giving only a passing glance,
but rather,
a man with a heart
who holds my gaze and
recognizes the person
underneath the illness.

Fingertips touch in a bridge
while elbows rest on the arms
of the chair,
two halves of his brain
taking in our conversation,
searching for clues
in the daily reports,
and unending tests,
sharing in my frustration
that answers are too slow
in coming.

His smiling eyes
behind glasses
tell me I have been heard.
Quirky comments
draw forth laughter and ease.

I know I am in good hands.

Lucky for me,
I have Sherlock Holmes
on my case
working diligently
to solve the mystery.

Wednesday, September 27th, Day 240

I started doing arm exercises today in physical therapy, adding to my already long routine of exercises. It usually takes me two hours to complete therapy. My knee is up to a 114-degree bend. I can feel the stiffness settle in on cold days.

My wound is leaking full-time again, at least eight dressing changes a day, the skin literally weeping for relief. Hopefully, the biopsy results from the endoscopy will be back tomorrow.

When I no longer have these doctors in my life, I will go through withdrawals. The attention of doctors has been instrumental in making me well, and I will miss the connection. It sounds silly, but I will miss playing the role of patient, maybe because that means it is time for me to become responsible for my own health again.

Friday, September 29th, Day 242

The news is in. I do have celiac disease. Sherlock talked to a world-renowned celiac specialist. He explained the situation, and the specialist believes the condition was brought on by the strep A infection. Basically, my immune system started eating away the lining of my gastrointestinal tract and caused this auto-immune disease. I will begin taking Prednisone, an anti-inflammatory medication in hopes it will cut down the drainage. At least I have an answer.

Wednesday, October 4th, Day 247

A few days on Prednisone and the drainage in my ileostomy has gone way down. However, I am still changing my dressing on my wound eight to ten times a day. Eating or not eating has little effect on the amount of drainage.

Without really talking to me about it, Dr. P stuck a tube in the fistula and attached a metal clamp to keep it in place. I tried to speak my mind, but the tube was out of the package and in my fistula before I could ask questions. I look freakish, as if I didn't before! Dr. P says he is not ready to do surgery.

I feel like a specimen, an experiment that has gone awry. Where are my rights as a patient? I know I need to speak up and be clear about what I need. A doctor with a listening ear would help a lot. I am done with dressings and tubes and doctors who are just as frustrated as I am because they don't have answers. I want all of this to end.

Taking Back My Power

Friday, October 6th, Day 249

I felt different talking to Sherlock at my appointment today. I was ready for answers. "This is it," I said. "I don't know what else to do. I'm very frustrated; nothing is changing. What are we going to do about this?"

I am starting on Prilosec, a potent medicine designed to cut down stomach acid. Sherlock said if this medication doesn't work in a week, he will talk to Dr. P about doing a localized surgery to cut out the fistula. It would be tricky, but Dr. P. might be willing to do it.

I talk to Sherlock like a family member and am not afraid to let him see and hear my frustration. I can't talk to Dr. P in the same way. I cry with Sherlock and tell him how my body hurts. I am no longer willing to settle for a "We'll see" answer. When I left today, Sherlock said, "I see, Jan, that you have reached the end. I get the point. I get the complete picture now. I understand." Just to be heard and understood made me feel like a real person again. I am no longer a *patient* patient.

DURING MORNING ROUNDS, ESPECIALLY IN THE EARLY months of my illness, it wasn't surprising for doctors to cheerfully show my belly to curious interns who had never seen a fistula. Seldom during the show and tell did a doctor think about my vulnerability. When the gown came up, the lower half of me was uncovered. I used to joke, if I had a dime for each time my crotch was exposed, I would be rich.

In the sterile environment of the hospital, it is easy to objectify patients, identifying a disease to treat. Most of the time, the doctor/patient relationship is about the diagnosis, procedures and protocol for making a patient well. And while some doctors made me feel less than human, it was still their voice I waited to hear each day with news of my prognosis. Doctors studied lab and test

MOVING MOUNTAINS | 217

results, searching for answers to the questions of my condition. They wielded power because they carried information—the latest results, interpretation of x-rays, etc. It was on their orders that drugs were administered, tests were prescribed, and progress was measured. Waiting for the powerful doctors became my daily chore.

I was thrown into relationships with doctors because of a devastating illness. Many of those who cared for me were young doctors with young children. If we had met somewhere other than the hospital, we shared common interests that could have turned into friendships. It was this commonality that brought us together, sometimes beyond the normal patient/doctor relationship. Looking at me, a young doctor might wonder what life would be like if his own wife was in my situation.

I was lucky to have doctors who treated me as a person first—doctors who would look me in the eye and talk to me, not to Tony or my mom. Often they would linger, share something about their own lives and then listen to my story—the frustrations, stories about the girls or concern for Tony. In these moments of sharing, the doctor's jacket and credentials disappeared and we became two people conversing, sharing a connection, a point in time. It makes sense that I would be drawn to these doctors—the one with the dry sense of humor, the one who remembered me on a trip to Mexico and brought gifts for the girls, the one who shared stories of his own children, the one who took the time to laugh with me, and did not forget that I was a person disguised as an illness. The human connection removed the sterility of the hospital and I experienced the acceptance of being fully human. What is more powerful—to cure or to make one feel human again? It is no wonder that these doctors, even though I haven't seen them in years, still hold a special place in my heart.

Monday, October 9th, Day 252

Sherlock told me to pull the tube from my belly because it wasn't doing any good. I called Dr. P in desperation and—using the little bit of power I was now claiming—said, "You have to help me. I know it's a pain; I know you've done it before many times and it still comes undone. But I need you to stitch up my belly."

When I went in to get stitched up, I told Dr. P that Sherlock would call him about the possibility of doing surgery on the fistula. Dr. P wrestles with this decision because it is such a complicated surgery. The wall of my intestine is nestled into my abdominal wall, and the whole section will have to be cut out. He is trying to salvage as much of my bowel as possible. Dr. P acknowledged that he can keep stitching my fistula because that part of my bowel will be cut away anyway.

I feel as if I spoke my mind with Dr. P. Even though we are still at the point of just stitching me up on a regular basis, at least I was heard. I can be a more active part of my healing now.

❧

I used to say, "Take me back to January 26th and let's start this year all over. Let's skip all this." I can't say that anymore because as much as I hate my wound, and am frustrated at the recovery process, I'm a different person. This has been a year of blessings amid tragedy. I have found love and care in the darkest of places.

Thank you, God. Stay with me and keep me going. Let the mustard seed faith of mine blossom into something beautiful. Thank you, Creator God. I couldn't have survived this year without the presence and prayers of thousands of people, especially those who know and love me. It is in You, Mother God, that I find the strength to face this wound every day. Love has given me the courage to survive.

Nothing Short of a Miracle

MY FRIEND JULIE REMEMBERS EXACTLY where she was standing in her kitchen that January when she got the call from Ginny. Words became tangled in the fear that rose in her heart. She just couldn't make sense of how Jan, ICU, and near death all fit into the same sentence. The more she mulled it over in her mind, the more confused she became. She called Ginny back and asked, "But what does this mean?"

> Miracles are an expression of love. The real miracle is the love that inspires them. In this sense, everything that comes from love is a miracle.
> - Marie Lloyd

"Nothing short of a miracle," Ginny replied. "Nothing short of a miracle."

The power of prayer—both spoken and said within our own hearts—is greater than we can imagine. Since we are made of energy, and everything around us affects our energy, it is no wonder that the prayers sent to me over that year changed my own vibration and created a web of healing around me.

I travel farther back in time to a first grade classroom, where Fr. Ken is blessing my neck. "Through the intercession of Saint Blase, bishop and martyr, may God deliver you from every disease of the throat and from every other illness." The saints and angels in heaven, as well as the saints and angels on earth, truly gathered and created the miracle of my life. Through all space and time, prayers traveled to deliver me from darkness and death. Even a prayer scarf from Mt. Everest was woven into the invisible net of support that raised me to life again.

This illness became a blessing in my life because of the person I became after the experience. I began to see life as the gift it really is.

So many times I asked God to show me how this illness would bring light into the world. Because of my experience, I was inspired to complete a Healing Touch Certification Program four years after my illness so I could facilitate healing in others, just as I had been the recipient of such healing.

In a recent healing touch session, divinely inspired words to a meditation floated out of my mouth, reminding both me and my client that God transforms our pain and makes beauty out of the ugly things in our lives. My own suffering connects me most deeply to others who struggle in their lives.

The truth is there are no ugly parts of our lives. If we shine light in the darkness, we find our challenges make us stronger. I wouldn't want to live it again, but I am forever grateful for the way our lives changed because of this experience. When we reach out through the pain in our lives, we can inspire others to transform their own pain into something beautiful. We all have the strength within us to move beyond fear into a place of peace. I help my clients see that changing our thoughts can change our lives.

Our lives are nothing short of miracles. Each breath we take, each time we walk or eat or hear another's voice—everything is extraordinary if we look with the eyes of gratitude and amazement. In the present moment, we may be suffering, but overall, there is amazing good in the world, and the older I get, the more often I choose to tap into the good and find unconditional love reaching back for me.

Tuesday, October 10th, Day 253

Come on! Seven dressing changes and the day is only half way through! Yesterday, I was so sure that love could help me survive anything, but today I am back in a place of despair. No explanation for all of this stuff! My attitude adjustment isn't working.

❧

I had my second session with a counselor who specializes in medical trauma. She hooked me up to the biofeedback machine, and immediately the meter hit the highest point, even though I thought I was relaxing. I am carrying all my stress, which prevents my body from healing.

The counselor told me to remember that I am a person with a wound, not just a wound. That struck home with me because my focus this past week has been the wound and not feeling like I am in control. I am a person who can say to the doctors, "What is it that I can do to become an active partner in my healing instead of sitting on the sidelines?" The doctors have been treating my wound, and now I will help them remember I am a person first.

Thursday, October 12th, Day 255

Sherlock told me to be straightforward with Dr. P. "To be truthful, Jan," he said, "I think he's afraid of what he is going to find in your abdomen and afraid of what the outcome might be."

What is the worst-case scenario if Dr. P goes in and operates? Will that worst-case scenario be any different in four to five months? Sherlock agreed that I'm in the best health I can be for surgery. Now that I am on Prednisone, my immune system becomes more compromised week by week.

I have to ask myself if I am prepared to hear what the results might be. What if Dr. P can't salvage my bowel? What if he has to take two more feet? Is that acceptable? Sherlock says no. The worst-case scenario would be to need TPN for the rest of my life.

Tony has agreed to go with me for my next appointment with Dr. P. Both of us are at the breaking point, ready to demand answers from Dr. P beyond stitches every few days. My skin and my psyche can't take anymore. We are going to ask him about his criteria for determining whether surgery is viable or not.

I'd like to be honest with Dr. P and say, "I trust you and trust your judgment. I know that when you do surgery, whatever the situation is, you will do what you can to the best of your ability, and that's all I can expect." I trust his abilities as a surgeon. I'm not sure I am ready to hear the worst-case scenario, but I am not willing to put up with the draining of this fistula for another three or four months unless there is a very good reason why.

Friday, October 13th, Day 256

We went to see Dr. P today. He walked into the appointment room and told us that it is time to schedule surgery. Tony and I just looked at each other, jaws dropped open. We had come armed for battle, and Dr. P just waltzed in and announced it was time. While I was there, he took the stitches out of the central line and also stitched up the fistula. I am going in for an upper GI on Tuesday. This is to triple-check that there is no obstruction in the bowel anywhere. We will be able to look at the x-ray and see the amount and the condition of the bowel. I am so relieved about surgery! Although Dr. P would rather wait, Prednisone became a factor. My immune system will only get worse as time goes on.

Dr. P says the worst-case scenario would be constant diarrhea because of lack of absorption or TPN for the rest of my life. However, he has known people with less than three feet of bowel, and they still manage. We will hope and pray that the bowel is not so adhered together with scar tissue that he has to cut it out. I know God will take care of me. I know God will guide Dr. P's hands when he operates.

Saturday, October 28th, Day 271

It's been a very long time since I talked. I feel like I should say, "It's been a very long time since my last confession!" Even though

I thought about picking up the tape recorder every morning, I couldn't bring myself to do it. I've been keeping all my feelings inside. My surgery is scheduled for November 8th. The end is in sight.

Right now, I have an intestinal bug, so not only is my wound leaking, I have increased ileostomy output. I am stuck at home lying on the bed, taking care of nothing but bodily fluids.

AT SOME POINT DURING THOSE LAST FEW WEEKS, WHEN the dressing changes became an hourly occurrence, I was too overwhelmed to pick up the tape recorder and share my thoughts. With the end in sight, I struggled with the dressing changes and another infection because I was ready to be on the other side of surgery. Yet, the questions haunted me. What if I had to be on TPN and not be able to eat for the rest of my life? I had struggled for months with this issue. What quality of life would I have if eating was not possible? As my body's strength to handle the daily grind wore down, my faith was completely tested. In one moment, I would recognize God working in my life, and in the next instant, I felt the well of my faith running dry.

Thursday, November 2nd, Day 276

It snowed last night, covering the ground with a light dusting of white and soothing my spirits with the calmness of winter. I received some long-distance healing touch from a friend because we couldn't drive to Ft. Collins. I have to believe that when I go into surgery, there will be so many people lifting me up to God that everything will be fine. I hope my plan and God's plan are on the same page.

I was talking to a friend at church today, telling her I doubt God would really want me to be on TPN for the rest of my life. But my plan isn't always God's plan, and God may see something redeeming in this that I don't see. My friend said, "You know, sometimes there isn't a lot of comfort knowing you're following God, is there?"

Yes, that's true, but God has been with me through this challenge and has wrapped me in Her loving arms many times. God will continue to be with me no matter what happens. I have heard the saying, "In the end everything will be okay. If it is not okay, it is not the end."

There is a surprising well of trust deep inside me that believes in a God who is looking out for my best interest. It is not like God snaps Her fingers and makes me well or throws trials in my path. I do believe people show up who are gifted in their skills to help me through the challenges. I have learned to see God in all the people around me, acting as the surgeon, the kind doctor who hears my cries, the countless people who raise me in prayer. I choose to see the blessings that make my life extraordinary.

Tony told a friend last night that we sometimes forget how far I have come. I remember when I was counting steps, not city blocks. I was stacking cones, not piles of laundry. Strength has returned to my fingers, arms, and legs without my noticing. I have traveled two steps forward for every one step back.

It will be a step back when I come home from surgery unable to do the things I am doing now. I'll be moving rather slowly, but

that's okay. I need that time to recuperate. Soon, I will be whole!
Monday, November 6th, Day 280

Happy Birthday, Hannah! Your wish is coming true. Soon I will have a new tummy!

I was hoping I wouldn't have to go back to see Dr. P to be stitched up, but I've been changing my dressing every 45 minutes. I can't do this for two more days. Knowing that surgery will take care of this nuisance is a comfort to me. I may get tired of having diarrhea, but at least it's something new.

Wednesday, November 8th, Day 282

The fistula is cursing me to the end. I just got out of the shower this morning, and it poured all over the floor. I changed my dressing, and in 15 minutes it was leaking all over. I had to change dressings again before I got to the hospital, and it is only 6:00 a.m.! I am not sad to see my nemesis go.

Hannah Helps Me Dress My Wounds

Saying Goodbye to Hannah at the College of St. Benedict

Recovery

I have sometimes been wildly, despairingly, acutely miserable...
but through it all I still know quite certainly that
just to be alive is a grand thing.

Agatha Christie

Whole Again

November 9th, Day 283

Before Dr. P took me into surgery, I said, "Do me a favor and don't keep the fistula." He laughed wearily, confirming that it had been a thorn in his own side.

Dr. P had the help of many prayers in surgery. His surgical resident told me they first cut out the wound and the fistula to remove all the scar tissue. They only had to take one-and-a-half inches of bowel with the fistula. The scar adhesions looked more like delicate spider webs than thick sinewy tendons. They took their time removing them so my intestines could move freely. And then Dr. P reconnected both parts of my bowel, so I no longer have the ileostomy.

This afternoon, we pulled the pressure bandage off my skin. I have tape blisters up and down the side of my wound now, and that is what causes pain. The incision is about 12 inches long from my rib cage down to my pubic bone. I thought I would have a bunch of little black stitches but I have actual staples, a silver row down my middle. They are ugly, and the skin is pulled very tightly, but I no longer have a draining belly! Wow!

I have walked twice today. The first time I used the walker just to make sure I had my balance, but I didn't use oxygen. When I walked with Tony this afternoon, I decided I didn't need the walker, so I left it in the hallway and continued walking. The only thing that hurts now is the movement in and out of bed because of the staples.

My heartburn last night was caused by the incorrect position of the NG tube. The nurses pulled it out seven inches, and 650 cc of fluid drained out in 10 minutes—no wonder I didn't feel good. The NG tube is in until I have bowel sounds. I hope to never have this tube down my throat again.

There is no joy in the routine of the hospital: 11:00 p.m.—vital signs; 2:00 a.m.—I am still awake; 4:00 a.m.—vital signs; 5:00 a.m.—blood draw. I told the night nurse that it's really great to come to the hospital to get some sleep. She said, "Why? Are you having trouble sleeping at home?" I had to explain that I was being facetious.

November 10th, Day 284

The NG tube is still in, but I am beginning to hear bowel sounds. The catheter came out, and I voided just fine. The best part about being here is seeing all the doctors and nurses who took care of me during my 100-day stay. They come in for friendly visits, no business, and that feels good. For a woman they brought back to life, they are happy to see me mending.

November 11th, Day 285

I just had my first "poop." It was diarrhea, but there was a solid mucus plug, and I feel so much better now. Hopefully, that means the NG tube will come out. I saved my stool so the nurse could see, just like when a toddler poops in the toilet for the first time. "Yes, that's pretty good," she responded.

November 12th, Day 286

Already, I am having bouts of diarrhea, but that means my system is working! I got to drink chicken broth for lunch today.

I have done a lot of walking. Sometimes, my stomach hurts. Yet, there really isn't much to complain about, compared to where I was.

November 13th, Day 287

I had a nice visit from Dr. G this morning. "My, you have grown taller!" he quipped. He was my infectious disease doctor, and I am sure he likes to see patients up and moving around.

I've had diarrhea all day, almost every 15 minutes. I had a couple bites of rice and carrots for lunch, hoping food will slow things down a bit.

When Dr. P visited, he looked at my belly and said, "You have a very svelte abdomen!"

I joked back, "It isn't worth what I went through to get it! Though it may be svelte, it sure isn't a lingerie type anymore."

The gift of humor carried me through many rough spots this year, and I am grateful I haven't lost my ability to laugh.

My ICU nurse Marsha came for a visit. Her eyes rimmed with tears when she told me one of her favorite "Jan" memories. She had been gone from ICU for a couple of days, and when she came back, I was the new patient. My nurse was Pat at the time, and she had been by my side all day and didn't have the chance to get away. Since Marsha had some time, she told Pat she would be willing to stay by my side, so Pat could take a break. Marsha came into the room and introduced herself, but stayed in the background. Mom and Dad were in the room, but no one was really saying much. Obviously, it was a very serious situation. She said my dad came up to me, brushed my hair aside, gave me a kiss on the forehead, and said, "I love you, Jan." She got so choked up that she had to leave. She says she will never forget all the love that was in my room. "You are so fortunate to have the family and support that surrounds you because most people would not have survived what you went through." Looking back over the year to a time that seems so long ago and realizing where I am today fills me with gratitude.

❧

For a little holiday spirit, I watched "It's a Wonderful Life" today. I have had a Jimmy Stewart experience. I don't know what people's lives would be like without me, but I do know that there are many people who have been touched by my story. At the very end of the movie, when the angel gets his wings and leaves a book for Jimmy Stewart, the inside cover says, "A man is never a failure when he has many friends." I think that holds true for me. My friends and family have been my support system. Their love and faith in me and Tony helped us survive day to day. This year has been a success because of them.

❧

I'm getting ready to go to bed now. I've probably had diarrhea at least 20 times today. Tonight, I am finally passing something other than water. I hope sleep will give my body a chance to revive. I knew I would have to go through this stage of diarrhea before getting better. It is just the next thing in my life that I have to overcome.

November 16th, Day 290

I get to go home tomorrow! I will use TPN at home, which is okay. At least I get to go home. My stomach is not upset anymore and I feel better. When I told Dr. P about the diarrhea he said, "We can always go back and disconnect you!" Fat chance of that happening! I will get better eventually. I trust that I will.

Sherlock does not want to increase my Prednisone unless he absolutely has to, so we're going to wait until Tuesday to decide, when I see him in his office.

I look forward to my own home and my own food. Hospital food is a pain. I thought it was ironic that the hospital didn't know what to serve me for a gluten-free diet. I am eating a lot of rice, hoping to slow down the movement of my digestive system.

There is a man who has been walking the halls at the same time I do every day. Today, when I passed him, he looked at me and said, "I envy you."

I replied to him, "Not too long ago, I was just where you are. Keep working!" I think God puts these people in my life to remind me to celebrate little successes and to remember how far I have come.

November 17th, Day 291

I love home! Becca ran in from school today and hugged me and wouldn't let go. Wrapped up in her love, I know that everything is right in my world.

November 18th, Day 292

Have I talked yet about the joys of having chronic diarrhea?

Today I have had five bouts of diarrhea instead of twenty! The day is only half over, but it is an improvement. I can't tell you what a joy it is NOT to be doing dressing changes!

November 20th, Day 294

Today, I listened to a friend share the challenges she was facing in her life. I instantly saw how my experience connected me to another person in pain. This connection is part of the good from this year. Still, to this day, I am overwhelmed by the number of people who continue to pray for me. Much of that support came by virtue of where Tony works and the visible position he holds in the church.

Last night I said to Tony, "I feel funny about the amount of prayers I've received because of the publicity around my illness." Tony asked me if I felt guilty. In a way, I do. Why did I deserve to have all the prayers of the entire church? That is a question I just can't answer. It humbles me that I was the recipient of so many people's prayers. The community of love around our family kept us going during all the rough spots.

THERE IS A CHINESE PROVERB THAT STATES, "A MAN who removes a mountain starts by carrying away small stones." Looking back on that year, I realize my only job was to carry away the stone that was in front of me each day. Some days were handled with much more grace than others.

Yet even when my own faith wavered, friends and family picked up their shovels and did the work of faith—each meal, each load of laundry, each friendly conversation was a small stone carried away with encouragement to bolster my own strength. I was continually inspired by others to keep walking the difficult path, doing the work of healing. The faith and strength of others carried me when I couldn't carry myself. Indeed, I am a living testament to the power of community. Together, as a community, we moved the mountain of illness and transformed it into a beautiful lesson in love.

November 22nd, Day 296

Yesterday, the big staples came out of my belly. Good thing that bikinis were out for me a long time ago!

Dr. P suggested I decrease the TPN, and Sherlock agreed, so I am down to 1000 cc a night. They really want me to get off the TPN altogether because the central line is a possible source of infection. The sooner it is removed from my body, the better.

I'm eating well, but we did increase the Prednisone again to help control the diarrhea. By the time I went to see Sherlock yesterday, I had been in the bathroom 13 times. He said that was just way too much. Hopefully, the Prednisone will help get the diarrhea under control. Despite the diarrhea, I am getting stronger every day.

November 24th, Day 298

Yesterday was Thanksgiving, and it was a wonderful, joyful, tear-filled celebration. It felt so good to be able to sit down with my family and eat a normal dinner, drink wine, and celebrate the

gift of life. Nothing poured out of my belly, and even though I'm
still dealing with the diarrhea, I'm keeping my fingers crossed
that things will slow down.

If the only prayer
you say in your life
is "thank you," it
would suffice.
- Meister Eckhart

I thanked Tony for doing such a fantastic job
with our little girls all year, keeping them healthy
and fed, and taking care of their emotional
needs. And I thanked him for being my rock and
strength, helping me to survive an unimaginable illness.

He looked at me through his tears and said, "I am just thankful
you are here."

"Me too," I cried.

November 30th, Day 304

Tonight is the first night since July 10th to be without TPN. I
have carried the backpack pump around with me for months, and
I almost don't know what to do without it.

Sherlock thinks I am eating enough to maintain even with the
diarrhea. I have started on a really nasty medication they give to
people with high cholesterol to bind the bile. He is hoping it will
help. It makes Metamusil taste like a party cocktail. Yesterday,
I only experienced eight times in the bathroom, so that is an
improvement.

December 1st, Day 305

The central line is gone! No more tubes sticking out of my
body. The first time in at least ten months that I have been free!
I actually bought a part of jeans so I could go out to a potluck at
church. It felt good to be wearing jeans, a sweater, and shoes, you
know, something a normal person would wear. No more sweats

all the time. It's funny how clothes are a sign of forward progress.

We had to wear name tags at the potluck. On the bottom of the name tag it said, "If I were an automobile, I would be…if I were an animal I would be…or if I were a plant I would be…" On my name tag I wrote, "If I were a plant I would be an artificial silk plant, because they don't die." I love to laugh whenever I can; this year was way too serious.

Tony says we've been in Advent for a year-and-a-half. First, we waited for the birth of Sarah, and now we wait for my healing. We are hoping to get back to normal soon! As I look upon this Christmas and holiday season and think about where I've been—and how far I've come—tears come to my eyes. I'm just so lucky to be here. Things could be very different for Tony and the girls, and I don't ever want to forget that. I don't want to forget how precious life is and what a gift it truly is to be living each and every day with people that I love. I hope this lesson does not fade over time, that the scars on my body will always be a telltale sign of where we've been and how far we have come.

December 8th, Day 312

On Monday, the home health service company picked up my IV pole and all the extra medical supplies. I no longer have a medical corner in my living room!

On Tuesday, Becca had her first Christmas concert. As I was getting Becca ready, she asked, "Mom, are you going tonight?"

I replied, "Of course I'm going!"

She smiled, "Oh good!"

"Aren't you glad I'm not in the hospital?" I asked.

She said, "Yes, but even better than that, you're getting to be a regular mom."

December 12th, Day 316

I went to see Dr. P today for the last time. I got the stitches out where the central line had been. When I left, I said, "Please don't take this the wrong way, but I hope I never have to see you as a doctor again!"

Sherlock called today to check on me. The diarrhea is about the same, and none of the medications we have tried seem to work. We will keep looking for a solution.

I am totally enjoying time with Sarah today. She is sitting on the bed with me, clapping and laughing. I finally feel like I am able to enjoy real mom activities. I never stopped being a mom, but so much other junk got in the way that I didn't have time to savor moments like this one.

December 15th, Day 319

My old place of employment called, and starting in January we will have to pay the Cobra price for insurance, which is about $250 more than we are paying now. My job is no longer there, which I knew. I don't have any idea how or when I will go back to work, but we will cross that bridge when it comes.

It's amazing how worried I was after I heard the news from work. All these terrible thoughts came flooding back. "What if we don't have enough money?" Have I already forgotten that God led us through an incredibly challenging year? Why should I worry about money? God will take care of us.

Christmas Letter to Friends and Family

Dear Friends,

We have jokingly called this year our year from hell. However, with reflection, we realize this has changed our lives for the better. Our experience deepened both our love and commitment to one another and developed qualities in us that have not always been prominent. On November 8th, Jan had her sixth and last surgery of the year. We are happy to report it was successful and we are beginning to see the light at the end of the tunnel in her recovery. She still has a lot of physical therapy and more digestive issues to endure, but that is minor compared to surgeries.

It has been a year of learning new things. For Jan, it was learning to do everything again, from walking to holding a pen and writing. For the rest of us, it was learning to deal with a serious illness in the family and finding the humor and the delight of new discoveries in spite of it. The girls always found enlightening things to say to alleviate some of the stress. Holding Sarah in her arms gave Jan comfort. Hannah (two-and-a-half), after giving Jan's hospital room a thorough cleaning, abruptly turned to Jan and said, "Mom, get up!" Becca (five years old) was the continual encourager, always noticing and pointing out improvements in Jan's condition. "Mom, you are standing by yourself!" "Mom, you are not using your cane." "You can bend over!" They were disappointed recently when they found out that Jan's belly button could not be saved during surgery. Becca was especially shocked that it would not grow back.

December 28th will be our ten-year wedding anniversary. There is much to celebrate and to be thankful for. We plan to take full advantage of our second chance at life. Again, we thank you for all your prayers over the year. In all of you, we came to see the face of God.

Merry Christmas!
Note from a couple at MPB

Dear Tony and Jan,

Merry Christmas to you and to your darling girls. Every time we see the two of you together with your children, we feel we are witnessing a continuing miracle—the miracle of healing in your life, Jan; the miracle of a young family's amazing faith—faithfulness and grace in the midst of incredible adversity; the miracle of physical and emotional strength given to a young husband to hold it all together with compassion, gentleness, and kindness day after day, month after month; the miracle of extended family and friends coming together to lend needed support; and the miracle of prayer offered from people not only at MPB, but from all over the country who heard your story and believed that God would bring about a miracle of healing. Your story and your faith have greatly impacted so many of us. Truly, you are a special family in whom God is revealed.

We wish you a wonderful Christmas and a good but DULL new year. May God continue to bless your family with health and happiness. We thank God for blessing our lives with you!

Happy Anniversary!

Happy Anniversary
Rita Mailander

Each year, as part of tradition, I select my own MOST ADMIRED man and woman of the year. I got the idea from Time Magazine. This year, you win my award. Your love, devotion, and dedication to one another deserve recognition. I wish I could give it to you on a national scale, but it's merely a local and personal award, and, unfortunately, brings no monetary stipend. I have been awed and humbled by your perseverance, faith, and stamina. You are a wonderful example of the goodness and power of God's love. I pray that power will heal and energize you in the new year.

It is an honor to know you. Happy Anniversary!

A New Beginning

January 4th, Day 339

Happy New Year, Jan!

We just got back from our time at the family cabin, where it is tradition to celebrate the New Year. This was a much better experience than our September trip. I loved participating in the games, the laughter, and the normalcy of activities. Even though I wasn't out walking the lake, I did get some great physical therapy walking the stairs to the bedroom. My weak right leg got exercise by having to stand on its own each time I climbed a step—one foot per step. Who knew I would be counting steps as a sign of progress!

Every morning now, I start my day with physical therapy. I ride the bike for 15 minutes and do my exercises. I go back to physical therapy tomorrow, and I will make sure I have a home exercise program that addresses all my needs. I want to do everything I can to strengthen my muscles.

I saw Sherlock on Tuesday, and I'm down to 30 mg of Prednisone. Next week, I will be down to 20 mg and then I will wean off Prednisone altogether. He is planning an endoscopy soon to see if there is still inflammation in my intestines. I've been up every night this week in the bathroom, and he thinks it is due to inflammation. Sherlock told me today that when my chart weighs as much as I do, he will discharge me! He said we only have about five pounds to go! I like the fact we can joke about this. He has seen me through a very difficult year. From giving me my first ice chips, to diagnosing celiac disease, to dealing with chronic diarrhea, he has never given up on me or gotten frustrated with me even when I came to his office and cried. He has been more than my doctor; he has been my friend—a friend who listens and cares about me and one who jokes with me. I am grateful for my Sherlock Holmes!

My Body Warrior

There is no longer a belly button to pierce,
as if the countless needle stabs weren't enough.

The belly button lost its life
in the brave battle
against the constant digestive juices
spewing from the fistula.

And although I no longer have
a football-sized wound on my belly,
I do have a 12-inch gully
where water likes to stream when I shower.

Countless scars cross my body,
from central lines and blood gas tracks,
to the dent in my thigh
where possible infection was thought to hide.
An old ileostomy crater
graces the side of my gully.

I am not entering a beauty contest soon.
Ever.

My breasts aren't big,
and my quads aren't the strongest,
and I have never kept
the dimple in my butt cheek.

Yet for all its flaws and battle wounds,
I love my body.

I love the beauty that shines from beneath
the skin and muscle and bones.
I love it for giving me a second chance.

January 13th, Day 348

As the anniversary of my illness approaches, I am beginning to reflect on the losses I have felt. For the most part, I am adjusting. But last night when Tony and I were sharing some quiet time, I cried and realized I have a lot of unnamed feelings, which is rare for me. I'm usually good at naming what is going on inside of me, but there have been so many losses, I haven't begun to sort them out.

One of the most difficult losses was intimacy with Tony. Illness creates havoc in all parts of life, and our sex life was directly affected. When people asked Tony what he gave up for Lent, he said, "I gave up sex this year, does that count?" I am reminded of a friend who, when working together on an engaged couple workshop, said that true intimacy takes place more in the vertical position than the horizontal position. I agree. We have strengthened our relationship, but that doesn't take care of the physical need.

We have to laugh at something that would otherwise be too painful. I am adjusting to my new body with signs that a war has been waged. "Don't my scars bother you?" I questioned Tony.

"No Jan," he replied. "Those scars may be on your body, but they're mine too." There is such meaning in that statement. I never carried the burden by myself the entire year. Tony was with me every single step of the way. Every surgery I had, he felt—in a much different way, but he was there. And every time

I was sick, every time I had to change a dressing and every time I was down, Tony felt that. What happened to me affected all of our family.

It was such a powerful statement of love that I was overwhelmed with a myriad of feelings all at once—thankfulness that Tony was there for me as well as sarcasm. "Oh yeah, right, like you really felt these scars. I'm the one who had to go through it all." But Tony had his own war to fight, and I don't know if I could've done what he did. Being a support person is as difficult, if not more difficult, as being the person going through the illness.

I also have a feeling of security knowing that I'm loved, no matter what, through anything. Tony's faith and trust in God, and his unconditional love for me, kept him anchored at my side.

There are many changes to come, much to grieve, and much to celebrate. Looking back is scary to see what we lived through and survived. Looking forward is daunting; knowing the road to full recovery contains unknown challenges.

But somehow, we will survive whatever life throws our way. We have the scars to prove it and the determination and love to walk this journey together!

LOOKING THROUGH MY BOX OF CARDS, I STOP WHEN I SEE watercolors splashed across a page. Hand-painted, the card draws my attention to its rainbow strokes, and the Rumi poem summons me to read.

Watch the dust grains moving
in the light near the window.

Their dance is our dance.

We rarely hear the inward music, but
we're all dancing to it nonetheless,

Directed by the one who teaches us, the
pure joy of the sun,
our music master.

The minute I heard my first love story
I started looking for you, not knowing
how blind that was.

Lovers don't finally meet somewhere.
They're in each other all along.

-RUMI

And then I read Tony's message:
Dear Jan,
You are the music of my life, the dance in my heart,
and the vision to see miracles everywhere.
Love, Tony

Maybe I was wrong. My love for my daughters wasn't
the only love holding me on this earth. Tony's love was
reaching through and beyond all the darkness, beckoning
me to continue the dance.

I fall in love with him all over again.

January 26th, Day 361
Sarah's First Birthday

I stand in the middle looking out at a complete year of my life and realize I have come full circle. The year started with the birth of Sarah and ended with a death—the death of an idea of what my life should look like. I stand here knowing that the adversity I faced made me a stronger person. Tony and I are a stronger couple, and with our children, a resilient family.

AT A SOCCER GATHERING YESTERDAY, ONE OF MY FRIENDS asked me if I missed Hannah and Becca now that they are at college. While I admitted that I enjoy not tripping over Hannah's backpack each day, and I like having a bed to sleep in when Tony is snoring, I do miss them terribly. My head tells me we have raised strong women who are making a difference in their own corners of the world, while my heart misses their laughter and their smiles. My favorite times always have been time spent with Tony and the girls. My friend said, "Of course you miss them. The Haas family is the embodiment of family. You are a unit and you function as a unit."

It was a great compliment to me and Tony for the way we have raised our family. Years ago, we sat down with the girls and crafted a mission statement to guide our lives together:

The Haas Family Mission

As a Family...

WE promise to respect, love, and nurture, as well as challenge each other to be our best.
WE promise to laugh, have fun together, and enjoy each other's company.
WE promise to look for God in everything, especially people.
WE believe our thoughts affect our words and actions, so we choose to be a positive influence on the world around us.
WE give thanks for all the blessings God has given us.

The original document bears each of our signatures as we pledged to one another to do our best in upholding our mission. Because of the challenges we have faced as a family, the bonds of love we share are strong, and they continue to reach across the miles to wherever our girls are, in whatever stage of their lives.

While Tony has taught the girls life lessons on the soccer field and through music, I have taught lessons through my relationship to self. I believe that having a good relationship with the innate wisdom that is always at our bidding can guide our lives. And while I may talk about the importance of self-care, I may not always show it. How true in life that sometimes we are the teachers, and sometimes we are the students. All three girls have learned well and will often quote wisdom back to me when I am not paying attention to the Divine messages in my own life. They are God's voice, gently leading me toward self-compassion and understanding. We are fellow travelers, each of us with gifts to share to make the journey light.

On Facebook the other day, Hannah typed this message: *Dear Sarah, I miss you. Love, Hannah.* It was so simple but its words spoke volumes about the genuine and true bonds of friendship the girls share. Tears flowed from my eyes, not only because I too miss Hannah and Becca, but because I know how richly blessed we are to have such amazing daughters, such wonderful teachers in our lives.

Pieces of Healing

April 2nd, Day 427

I had a check-up with Dr. M today. He is very pleased with my progress and is happy to clear me for part-time work. He said my personality is even back to normal. I asked him what he meant.

"When you were sick in the hospital, no matter what kind of question I asked, you would always turn and look to the people who were in the room with you and expect them to answer. Even if it was as simple as "How are you?" you wouldn't answer. I think your biggest challenge as you go back to work is not the physical wear on your body, but the emotional and mental piece of working again. It is the self-confidence part, because when you are a sick person, you become dependent on others for everything. Now, it is a matter of becoming independent again and accepting where you are—being confident that you can do something."

MY SENSE OF SELF WAS LOST IN THE MIDST OF TRAGEDY. It was easy for me to slip into the role of a victim, the victim of a strange, rare illness. There was no thought involved in letting others be responsible for my care. Building my self-confidence again came in pieces as I began to manage the daily challenges of my life.

Even now, there are days when I search for a lost sense of self in the midst of obstacles. There are times when I bring all of my story and my pain into the here and now. I convince myself that I am the only one with problems and I am the only one who struggles to get back in balance. Occasionally, I think I would like to slip into ignorance and not know the truth—that no matter what the circumstances of my life, I am the only one responsible for how I feel and how I show up in the world. It is up to me to create a meaningful future. And I can only do that when I decide to live in the present.

Even illness is full of light. If there is a word that has echoed over and over again in my head and in my heart as I have walked this journey, that word would be *trust*. I continue to develop trust in my own abilities. I trust I am in the right place at the right time and whatever experience I am having is the right one. Each difficulty in life presents me the opportunity to learn something new about myself. Amazingly, light shines brightest when it is surrounded by darkness. I search to find God, who is always in the present moment.

There is a quote that says, "If you teach what you most need to learn, you can shift faster." God must delight in me saying I am a Balance Coach, educating and encouraging others to live a healthier life through education and awareness. I find strength for my own continued journey when Divine words are shared with another in conversation and my inner voice asks me if I am listening.

April 28th, Day 453

Tony and I arrived at our married roots—St. John's University in Collegeville, Minnesota—where spring has yet to take hold of the land. It is warm, high 50s, and already dark. We didn't get a chance to see a sunset over our favorite cross in the cemetery, but we will. It feels so right to be back here—the simplicity, the silence, the beauty, the peacefulness, the strong, sturdiness of the place. Yes, there is strength here. I know that if we are to find peace with what happened last year, this will be the place to do it.

The chime of the clock and the ringing of the banner bells remind me of our early married days when life was simple—our little apartment, studying, and passing the time with laughter and friends. There was no sadness. It is a place to reflect on the sadness and challenges of the past year, but also to remember the joy that came out of such darkness. Our journey home has begun.

Speak to me, Creator God
in the quiet of my heart.
Let all creation sing your joy.
I hear the simple sound of the songbird,
the stirring of wind through the pines,
water lapping at lake's edge.
The loon calls over the cold water,
and the sound of bells vibrate
like a heartbeat within.
Speak to me of peace.
Great are your ways, Oh God.
Make your path known to me.

Sit with me in quiet conversation.

As we shared our story, our private retreat leader told us that we had just been through a year of grace. Many people would have chosen the path of anger. "Why? Why did this happen to us?" But we chose a different route—asking God to be with us through it all, to not leave us alone in the darkness. In the midst of the worst thing we have ever experienced came a love so deep and healing, and we are forever changed. For all the grace in our lives, I am full of gratitude.

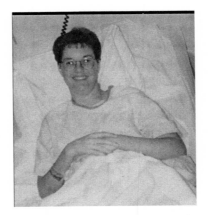

The Smile Says it All: I am Whole Again!

The Family Celebrates with Me by Riding
Up and Down on the Hospital Bed

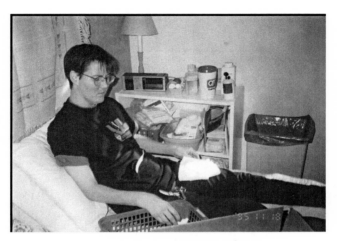

Putting Away the Last of the Medical Supplies

The Butterfly Pavilion in December: My
Prednisone Face, and Tired Girls Show
the Wear of a Very Challenging Year.

Tony and the Girls are the Light of my Life! August 2011
www.Turpenoff.com

EPILOGUE
+In Memoriam
Remembering Dr. Ken Weiner

Dr. Ken Weiner,
Gastroenterologist and Friend

He came to me in a dream. I hadn't seen him for well over a year and was so sad to hear of his death in August of 2009. I wasn't able to attend the funeral.

He was my Sherlock Holmes, the doctor who spent countless hours on my case, searching for answers to bring relief to my constant digestive problems. And here he was in my dream, as real as in life.

"I have to find a new doctor," I said to him, "because you died on me!" I could feel my anger boiling up over the sadness that lay beneath the surface.

After a moment or two, he said, "You know, you wouldn't even talk to me when I first met you."

"That is because I was in a coma, on a ventilator, and had a tube stuck down my throat!"

He smiled.

Side by side we walked and talked, remembering the jokes we shared during that difficult year, a little laughter to break the seriousness of the situation. His smile and kind words were balm for my soul, if not for my broken body. After that year in the hospital, I saw him less and less, but I would still leave his office with a fondness in my heart, as if I had just left coffee with a dear friend. He too had three children, and every time we talked about some new medicine or treatment, his barometer was whether or not he would put his own wife on a certain protocol. His thoughtful consideration of all possibilities was one of his best gifts. He trusted me to know my own body and what it needed, even when we were at a loss for what the best course of action might be.

In a peaceful pause from our banter, I said, "You know, I was so sorry that I didn't get to say goodbye."

He stopped walking, turned toward me, and putting his hands on my shoulders, turned me so that I faced him. He looked me in the eye and said," I love you, Jan."

What does one do with such a gift? Was this his way of continuing his never-ending encouragement? Was it also a way of acknowledging that patients are important to doctors, and not just the other way around?

Tears fill my eyes as I ponder the mysteries that are beyond human understanding. No matter how it happened, I am grateful for the gift and am happy I got to say goodbye to a man who helped me regain my health. Even if it was in my dreams.

As a wise person named Dumbledore once said to a wizard named Harry Potter, "Of course it is happening in your head, Harry, but why on earth should that mean that it is not real?"

A Conversation with the Author, Jan Haas

"The truth is that our finest moments are most likely to occur when we are feeling deeply uncomfortable, unhappy, or unfulfilled. For it is only in such moments, propelled by our discomfort, that we are likely to step out of our ruts and start searching for different ways or truer answers."

Unknown

1. In your story, we leave you still struggling with diarrhea. What has happened with regard to your health challenges since your illness?

The years following my illness were incredibly challenging. Reading over my journals during that time, I saw the continued struggle to find wholeness. I sought new therapies, new foods, and new supplements, all in the effort to help my digestive system return to a sense of normal. Sherlock suggested I might have to be on Prednisone my whole life. Tony asked him if he would allow his own wife to take Prednisone for the rest of her life, and he said no. Even though Sherlock was part of the allopathic medicine field, he became one of my best advocates, telling me to trust my body and do what worked. He encouraged me to search for alternatives.

One adventure carried me 12 hours to Sedona, Arizona to see a doctor who told me if I wanted to get well, I would return to him each month. I tried all kinds of supplements, many of which were too harsh on my 12 inches of colon because of their cleansing properties. I continued searching for relief from the relentless diarrhea that plagued me.

Tony voiced his concern that I was searching for a miracle cure, one I might never find. I would have to learn to accept things the way they were. I expressed to him I just wanted to be happy. Little did I know then how important it was to accept my current state of life to find happiness and healing.

2. Physically, what have you lived with and what have you learned to accept?

In the first years after my illness, it was normal for me to be in the bathroom ten times a day. Despite that, I managed to go back to work in an office as a benefits coordinator. Then, in December, four years after my initial hospitalization, I returned to the surgical ward for one scheduled and one emergency surgery because of an obstructed bowel. Luckily, the surgeons had to cut out less than five inches of bowel. During the recovery period, I made a promise to myself: eight abdominal surgeries are more than enough for any one lifetime. Shortly after my hospitalization, I tried a new supplement that drastically cut down my time in the bathroom. Finally, I felt there was a light at the end of the tunnel.

I look back now and see how each doctor, each supplement, brought me closer to being healthy again. Each piece of the puzzle led me to a greater understanding of the mind-body-spirit connection, and I believe that has helped me maintain my health. Good supplements, a healthy diet, and my persistence created a new normal for me. I have worked at becoming a friend to my body, treating it well and trusting it to carry me through the difficulties of life.

Even still, my short digestive system lends itself to times when I need to be close to a bathroom. Within a few moments of arriving at a destination, I scope out where the bathrooms are. When we travel, I time my eating so that we will stop at the right time. I could write a book on the best restrooms across the Midwest.

Although my body is different, my faith and sense of humor have allowed me to adjust to a new way of thinking. Bad days lend themselves to the appreciation of rest, and I when I slow down, I can focus on the gift of being alive. I journal and listen to the messages my body is sending. Sometimes, though, I still have to remind myself to be grateful for the gift of waste elimination!

I never needed surgery on my knee. Physical therapy and normal activities such as walking stairs helped me gain full motion and flexibility again. Despite all of my health concerns over the years, Tony and I found and enjoy intimacy again. I feel so fortunate to have walked this journey with an incredible life-giving man.

3. This year of illness took place between 1995 and 1996. Why did you wait until now to share your story?

This story has been aching to be told for 16 years. I tape recorded my thoughts all those years ago because I knew I wanted to write a book. In the first couple of years after my illness, my journals reflect my yearning to make the book a reality. Yet, the job of motherhood took precedence over the role of writer. If I had attempted the book while my girls were young, I wouldn't have been the type of mother I have lived to be.

When I came back from death's door to be a mother to my children, I didn't think about how one day they would go off to college and lead their own lives. I only thought about being a mom who would snuggle in with little girls on the couch, read bedtime stories, laugh at their silly jokes, and lavish them with love. It was a selfish move on my part. I didn't want to miss any of their childhood.

Now that two daughters are away at college and the third is two years away from leaving, I feel my roles shifting—balancing motherhood with writing and speaking; a woman ready to share her gifts beyond the scope of family.

If I had written this book in Jan's time, the book would be empty of the wisdom that only time and healing brings. I was surprised by the emotions that hit me as I wrote each section of the book. Working through those emotions gave me a window into the past experiences through which I could see to write meaningful reflections. As I worked through each emotion, I found myself with a better understanding of where I was then and how it relates to my life now. The year of illness continues to share its lessons. Why am I continually surprised when God's time is always the right time?

4. *You just said that your year of illness continues to share its lessons. Is there one lesson that stands out for you above all the others?*

The biggest lesson is simply having gratitude for my life. Standing on the top of a mountain in Grand Lake, Colorado last September, I had a 360-degree view of the world around me. In the late fall afternoon, with the sun burning brightly in a rich blue sky, long mountain shadows stretched across my view. The deep forest of the evergreen trees made a stunning backdrop for the aspen that were turning gold. Fiery orange and red dotted the mountain, turning the whole scene ablaze with color. Even the pine beetle kill, though abundant, was part of the beauty around me. Its rust-colored damage blended into the rich colors of fall, and in the bigger picture, the splendor couldn't be dimmed by Mother Nature's madness.

I had just spent three days alone at the family cabin working on my book. I was in awe of my life. I held my arms in the air and expressed praise to the Creator of the Universe, to the Master of Love. I was keenly aware of the miracle of life. I remembered back to 1995 when I wanted to stand on the mountain and shout, "Why me?" Now I proclaimed, "God is good! My life is abundant and overflowing. Thank you! Thank you! Thank you!"

5. You share at one point in your story how you were ready and willing to give up, but you chose to fight. Do you still fight to live?

In the throes of illness, it occurred to me how easy it would be to let go and allow death to take me. At that time, fighting against all odds was necessary for me to live again.

However, in the act of daily living, I can no longer fight to live. Now, letting go means giving up the illusion of control and allowing the flow of life to carry me. When I fight to be in control, everything I resist continues to plague me. When I fight Perfectionism, she fights back. When I sit in Judgment, Judgment criticizes me more. When I find Compassion, she flows out into the world and creates compassion for each person I meet.

In a talk I gave the year after my initial illness, I talked about a geode as a metaphor for my life. It was only after I was broken open that I saw the beauty within myself, and God's love was able to shine through all the darkness. Flowing with life doesn't mean avoiding pain, but rather embracing it as a teacher and moving forward with newfound wisdom.

6. *There are many themes running through your book; community, faith, trust, family, and love, to name a few. What is the most important message you hope people take away after reading your book?*

If there was only one meaning to glean from the pages of this book, it would be that we are never alone. God casts a wide network of saints, angels, and everyday people to walk with us and sometimes carry the burden. If we open our eyes, we can see the work of many people carrying small stones and moving the mountain that is before us. Sometimes, God shows up in doctors and nurses, a mother's care, a daughter's voice, a husband's unending love. God may look like a community of people helping to make one young family's journey a little easier. As Pearl S. Buck says, "God is always present. Most people just don't recognize Him." As you move your own mountains, my prayer is that you open your eyes to see how God reveals love in your own life. And may you find the act of moving mountains

Acknowledgments

While this book tells my story, my story is just a thread running through a greater tapestry that incorporates all the people who have touched my life in some way. And as a single thread, this story would not have unfolded or been as rich without the support and love of many people. Together, with their input, we have made a beautiful weaving.

First, I would like to thank my husband, Tony, who has believed in me from the very beginning. His love, patience, and understanding have allowed me to write and follow my path. Thank you and I love you.

Without my mother's journal, there would have been no way to tell the initial story of my hospitalization. Her journal recorded the pain, fear, and darkness the family encountered in the initial days and then months of my illness. Not only am I grateful for her written words, but also for the insightful conversations and friendship we share. I love you!

Because of the contribution from my early readers, this story's reflections are a powerful addition to the journal written many years ago. Carol Sullivan reignited the story spark with a journal workshop and then shared great writing and editing tips. I know the journal workshop took place at the right time in my life. Brenda

Foster and Kelly Gaul, nurses from my days in the hospital, helped me clarify the medical pieces of the story and shared their own experiences in community pieces and the foreword. Kathy McGovern asked me to share more of the pre-story so you could get to know who I was before the illness. Darleen Benson , Andrea Costantine, Susan Grubaugh, Jay Heinlein, and Emily Saunders all supported my writing process. All of these early readers braved the original raw copy and gave brilliant suggestions to make the story read more smoothly. Thank you for your honesty and willingness to be a part of my healing journey. You made the work of writing much easier.

I am thankful for all the stories from community members, both the published and unpublished narratives that reminded me no one suffers alone. I look forward to the many more stories that will be shared as a result of this book.

To Donna Mazzitelli, my editor, who through this process became a great friend and mentor. She is the midwife who held my hand and helped me labor through the last stages of birthing this story. Thank you!

My love and gratitude goes out to Andrea Costantine, who became my walking buddy, my layout artist, and a very dear friend. Her light shines brightly, giving me strength to continually step out in faith and stand in my own power.

Finally, by the grace of God, I thank St. Blase, who not only delivered me from disease, but by the blessing of my throat gave me the courage to speak my truth, write this book, and allow others to share in my experience. It is my hope that others who are experiencing their own mountain of darkness will find hope in its pages.

About the Author

Jan Haas is a teacher, wellness coach/mentor, speaker and writer. She is a contributing author in the women's anthology *Speaking Your Truth*, *Volume One*. This is her first full length book.

She lives with her husband and family in Denver, Colorado. Spending family time in the mountains is one of Jan's great joys. She also likes to read, walk and spend creative time in the kitchen.

Visit Jan's blog at www.janhaas.com